PASTRIES FROM THE PAST

From my Grandmother's Recipe Book

JUDITH GURFINKEL

Co-Producer Leora Steif

Impleo

ਅਮਨਦੀਪ ਸਿੰਘ 1/16/2023
604-307-4176

PASTRIES FROM THE PAST

Copyright © 2022 by Judith Gurfinkel

All rights reserved. No part of this book may be reproduced in any manner whatsoever without written permission except in the case of brief quotations embodied in critical articles and reviews.

First Printing, 2022

ISBN 978-1-7776544-2-9 (paperback)
ISBN 978-1-7776544-3-6 (epub)

Cover design and photography by Judith Gurfinkel

Impleo Systems
2006 West 15th Ave
Vancouver BC, V6J 2L5
Canada
info@impleo.ca

Contents

Preface		1
1	Introduction	3
2	Cream Cakes	13
3	Nut Cakes	35
4	Puddings	54
5	Cookies	69
6	Coffee Cakes	85
7	Fruit Cakes	100
8	Strudels	113
9	Salty Pastries	125
10	Grandmother Ilona	133
About The Author		146

Preface

This book has 40 recipes of cakes, sweet and savory baked goods and desserts I have selected from the yellowing, 80-page notebook my grandmother kept through her life. It is a book about the art of baking as it was practiced by a dedicated housewife in the early 20th century, at the height of the Austro-Hungarian Empire until WWI, in Budapest between the wars, and the years after WWII under the communist regime in Hungary.

My grandmother, Ilona Adler, was born in 1886 in a Slovakian small town, then part of Austro-Hungary. She married in 1904, at the age of 18, and started collecting recipes as she began her married life with my grandfather. The recipes are in German and Hungarian, as she was fluent in both languages from her bilingual background.

Reading the recipes and experimenting with baking was a thrill for me and it presented a great insight into the ingredients, tools and baking conventions in Austro-Hungarian traditions of that bygone era. Also, it is my way to commemorate grandmother's life and my father's family.

Ethnic groups in Austria-Hungary, 1910

My grandmother died in 1976 in Antwerp, Belgium. Among her belongings was this recipe notebook, which I received many years later from my cousin Georges. It took me a couple of years to decipher the content and translate the recipes to English, which presented me with great challenges. The German language has many different words for mixing and whipping, according to intensity. The same goes for grinding nuts - is grinding pounded, crushed, grated, ground or finely ground? And then there are the names of ingredients that do not exist today in our everyday or names not used anymore in the modern German.

Grandmother Ilona, 1904
JG

This book includes a selection of the successfully tested delicious cakes and pastries from the 300+ recipes in the notebook. After the recipes were translated from German and Hungarian to English, they were carefully tested and adjusted to current units of measure, ingredients and tools. The testing and detailed instructions were provided by my friend Leora Steif.

My grandmother's notebook has many pastry recipes not included in this book. I did not include all the laminated dough recipes, doughnuts and a variety of desserts made with quark (*topfen*) – maybe in a next version. For each recipe, I included a copy of the original page from the notebook with the text and the direct translation, for reference, and tried to keep the adapted instructions short and simple.

The recipes are organized into 8 sections: **Cream Cakes** – for people who like their cakes with cream, like my husband. **Nut Cakes** – as the notebook had surprisingly many recipes based only on almonds, hazelnuts, chestnuts without any flour or breadcrumbs, I decided to have a section for all the people in my family with gluten free diet. **Cookies** – of course are for my grandkids to bake together or treat them. **Puddings** – are my new discovery. The notebook has a variety of puddings and for me it was a novelty. **Coffee Cakes** and **Salty Pastries** – are for occasional entertainment, family gatherings and get together with friends. Or just for a bite with morning coffee. **Fruit Cakes** – we tried a few fruit recipes from the notebook, one for the fruit of each season. And of course, **Strudels** – the most quintessential Austrian / Hungarian dessert.

I

Introduction

Recipes of the past are very different from the detailed recipes we are used to today. Each recipe has a few lines with the ingredients, their quantities and some hints about the preparation process. The title of the recipe frequently reveals a lot about the result: its shape, purpose or tradition. An experienced baker, like my friend, Leora, had to check the translation and apply her baking skills, sometime by trial-and-error to turn the recipe into a successful pastry. With the adapted recipe from Leora, I tried it, once or twice, until I reached a tasty and decorative result, to the delight of my family and also to take a photo for this book.

We were surprised by the number of eggs and amount of sugar used in the recipes and the sheer volume size of some of the cakes. In some recipes, we had to work with half the instructed quantities and in most recipes, we reduced the amount of sugar drastically.

Special difficulty understanding in each recipe were the confusing units of measure used along the pages of the recipe notebook, the unfamiliar tools or ingredients mentioned and lack of specificity regarding the time and temperature required for each step of the baking process.

Units of Measure

Among the interesting aspects of the recipes was the research into the variety of old units of weight and volumes mentioned in the recipes. In the 19th and early 20th century Austro-Hungary's and Bohemia's official units of measures varied according to ethnic and geographical identity of the population. Many recipes have dekagram (dkg) as the commonly used unit of weight, but many others have pound *Pfund*

or *Lat* (*lath*). They even used some medieval Hungarian measurements like *Itze* and *Lót*. It seems that my grandmother collected the recipes from her friends and relatives, using various units and they were all acceptable and used interchangeably.

Most recipes follow the Austrian conventions of dekagram (dkg or deka) as the commonly used unit of weight, and other's have pound (*Pfund*) or methods like a cup or a handful, walnut size or fist size etc. Or use *Lót*, a medieval Hungarian measurement of weight, approximately 17.5 grams or 1/32 pound.

Pfund
JG

The gram equivalent to a pound is not very clear as it has changed during the centuries and varied between regions. In 1761 the Empress Maria Theresa tried to standardize the measures and weights of the Habsburg Monarchy to be one *Pfund* (16 ounces) equals 560.012 grams. A later reform, in 1816, defined a uniform civil *Pfund* to be equal to 467.711 grams.

Balance scale
JG

In some recipes the weight is defined in relation to the weight of the quantity of eggs, using a balance scale, popular in every Austro-Hungarian household. For example, the instruction for using flour "4 eggs heavy" means 4 eggs in the left tray to balance against the amount of flour in the right tray.

Another puzzle was to figure out what was the weight of a bar of chocolate in 1920? We assumed 70 grams, based on research into chocolate bar producers of the early 20th century, like Lindt and Fry's.

Liquids are measured mostly in litres, sometimes *Seidl*, cup or spoon (caffe spoon, cream ladle or soup spoon). Also, a medieval Hungarian liquid measurement is used - the *Itze* (also *Icce*) which is approximately 0.8484 liters or 3 1/3 cups and *Meszely* which is 1/2 *Icce*.

Certain recipes mention a *Stamperl*. What exactly is a *Stamperl*, I wondered? After research, I found out that it is a small schnapps glass that in Bavaria and Austria, measures 2 cl (20 ml) or 4 cl for the "double" drink. Usually, it was a cylinder-shaped glass with a solid bottom and thinner walls.

For weight measurement in this book, we used grams and assumed that 1 pound is equal to 500 grams. Other weight units we exchanged to grams by calculating and finally adjusting by trial and error. When solid ingredients are specified by their volume, we tried to apply our common sense and imagination.

Stamperl
JG

Time and Temperature

The recipes are very vague about the baking time of cakes and pastries.
Usually, the recipe would say: "bake until pink" or "bake until ready". Apparently because ovens must have been very different in each household. As well, experienced housewives could judge by themselves when the baking is ready.

On the other hand, mixing, whipping and cooking times, are very specific. For whipping or kneading it is usually between ½ to a whole hour. A popular baking method in the notebook is steaming – when the baking form is immersed in a pan of water inside the oven, usually, for this method the time is specified for ¾ hour or longer.

The recipes have no instruction as to the baking temperature. Sometimes it can say "bake slowly" or "in a hot oven". Presumably, the oven technology available then had no exact temperature dials....

Sparherd
JG

The economy stove, *Sparherd,* is mentioned a few times in the recipe book, so after some research found out what a momentous invention it was. Developed late in the 18th century, the stove had a smoke jacket that became customary during the 19th century and so the use of open fire in the household gradually disappeared. The main purpose of the economy stove was to reduce the energy consumption when cooking and baking. Thanks to the closed firing system, with an ash grate and flue pipe in the chimney, the kitchens became smoke-free and since the beginning of the 20th century, newer versions were enameled to allow easy cleaning to emphasize the cleanliness of the kitchen. On the front of the stove there are two flaps for firing, ventilation and cleaning on the right with the ash pan at the bottom, next to it the larger oven door. With the burners, the cast-iron stovetop allowed controlled cooking of several dishes at the same time, even in a small household.

Technics and Tools

The breadth and variety of baking expertise are evident in those recipes. For example, the complicated recipe of the Punch Cake (notebook page 50) includes all 3 types of cake batter, which differentiates the ingredients in each type of batter, be it Sponge, Genoise and Chiffon:

- **Sponge:** The sponge batter contains no fat other than that occurring naturally in egg yolks, and the yolks and whites are usually beaten separately.
- **Genoise:** With a genoise, melted butter is used to enrich the batter, which is made by beating whole eggs, sometimes with additional yolks, together with sugar, over warm water.
- **Chiffon:** The chiffon cake is a hybrid of the sponge and the genoise. The addition of oil gives

this cake its characteristic moist and tender texture. The yolks and oil are beaten into the sugar, flour and other dry ingredients including a leavening agent (not normally used in the other two cakes). The whites are whipped separately and then folded into the mixture.

	Sponge	**Genoise**	**Chiffon**
Texture	Moist and springy	Crumbly, airy, moist	Moist, light, fluffy
Eggs	Egg yolks and whites are beaten separately	Whole eggs are beaten together. Additional yolks are sometimes added.	Egg yolks are beaten with oil, sugar, flour, and other dry ingredients. Egg whites are whipped separately.
Unique ingredients	—	Clarified butter	Oil
Leavening agent?	No	No	Yes

Sponge, Genoise and Chiffon Cakes
JG

The recipes include instructions how to get air better into the batter and keeping it in for the lightness of the cake: by beating eggs longer (up to half an hour) and beating the yolks with sugar separately from the whites, at room temperature, or by beating over a saucepan of simmering water.

The use of yeast seems to be very proficient, detailed and easy to follow. In a recipe on notebook page 76, the instruction for the quantity of yeast to be used is "use the amount you can buy for 2 *Krajczár*" (1/100 of the *Krone*). The use of baking powder to make the dough light and loose is mentioned only in the later pages of the recipe notebook.

Some recipes call for boiled egg yolks pressed through a sieve and added to the cake or cookie batter. It seems to be an old European secret to make incredibly tender baked goods. I tried, and surprisingly, it works. The Linzer cookies turned out incredibly delicate.

The strudel dough is the stuffed pastry most popular in all regions of the Austro-Hungarian Empire. There are a few strudel recipes in my grandmother's notebook with various fillings – apples, almonds, cream and poppy seeds. The strudel dough is not the puff pastry that we use today, bought from the store, it is very different and quite easy to make.

My grandmother's kitchen must have been equipped with a variety of baking pans and forms, trays and tins, cake rings of various sizes and specialty forms like the *Rehrücken* - "saddle of venison" form. Other tools mentioned in several recipes are different cookie cutters and unique purpose bowls.

My own authentic Hungarian mortar
JG

Baking was a lot of physical effort as they did not have electrical appliances like mixers and food processors. The mixing, whipping and beating instruction are 30 to 60 minutes long. All the grinding and crushing of nuts was done by hand in a mortar or other manual grinding and milling equipment.

Ingredients

The recipe notebook is surprising by the richness of the ingredients it lists. There were years of abundance and years of shortages during the 20th century. The years before WWI were years of wealth and excess, suddenly ending with the difficult war years. Between the wars, until WWII were years of prosperity, but there came the great recession and then again, recovery. I wonder, how available all these ingredients were through the century.

My grandmother's cakes are made of a variety of ground nuts and flour. It seems that nuts and nut flour was readily available, more than wheat flour. Therefore, many cakes are made of exclusively with nuts, sometimes mixed with some breadcrumbs or mixed with flour. Some pastry recipes have also rice flour or potato.

The number of eggs used in the cakes is astounding. I wonder if the eggs of those days were smaller than what we have today. Some recipes use 10, 12 or 16 eggs for the dough and then even more for the cream. It is not rare to be left with a few egg whites because the dough used more egg yolks than whites.

My grandmother had recipes to solve that problem and use the egg whites. For example, the recipe for Bishop's Bread allows to add your spare egg whites to the batter. Or the Snow Cake that is made only with egg whites.

The variety of sugar types was also surprising. I know that in Europe it is quite easy to find in stores all kinds of sugar, but not so in Canada. When the recipe says "sugar", we assumed granulated sugar. They measured sugar by grams or by cubes. And all the recipes have a lot of sugar, to make the pastries too sweet for our taste, so we cut back on the amount of sugar radically. Some recipes have Vanilla Sugar, Pearl Sugar, Powder (confectioners') Sugar or Caster Sugar. When feasible, we found substitutes in our adapted recipes.

- Vanilla Sugar is confectioners' sugar that has been infused with vanilla flavour. It is difficult to find in stores but easy to make at home.
- Caster Sugar is finely granulated sugar – between the granulated and the confectioners' sugar. In North America it is called "superfine sugar" or "berry sugar". Its advantage is that it dissolves quickly, especially perfect for meringue and whipped cream.

- Pearl Sugar (*Hagel Zucker*), also known as nib sugar and hail sugar, is coarse, white and used extensively for baking throughout Europe. As the grains do not melt at typical baking temperatures, they provide a beautiful crunch when sprinkled on cakes and biscuits.

Perl/ Hail sugar
JG

Butter comes also in different qualities, according to its fat content. Most recipes do not specify the butter quality but some mention "Tea Butter" for the best butter quality. We wondered why tea? There are a few theories. After some research it turned out had nothing to do with the word "tea", but it is an abbreviation of

Austrian Teebutter
JG

"Teebutter". The best butter of the Monarchy was made in the dairy farms of Archduke Frederick of Teschen in Silesia, and from 1895 it was marketed under the brand name TE.E. (Teschener Erzherzögliche Butter) to become a common name for good quality butter. Another theory links the name to the Schärdinger brand, founded in 1900 as the "First Austrian Central Tea Butter Sales Cooperative", which had as their emblem a teapot.

My grandmother's pantry, I assume from the recipes, had many different spices. The recipe notebook mentions vanilla, usually from the pod, sometimes cinnamon, cloves, anise and carraway seeds. Maybe my grandparents had a wine cellar too. The recipes use wines, liquors, and rum generously.

Chocolate was measured sparingly; it must have been expensive back then. The recipes instruct the use of chocolate by bars - *Taferl*. It raised the question what was the weight of a bar. After some research into the history of chocolate production in Europe, we concluded that it must have been 70 grams.

Alkörmös
JG

The recipes mention a variety of fruits, local cherries and plums, local apple brands and tropical fruits, like oranges, *Pomeranz* (*Seville* or bitter orange), and dates. There is a local fruit called *Alkörmös*, to use as color additive to make pink batter. The English name for this plant is "pokeweed berry". Its juice was used in the past for liquor and food coloring. Now it has been banned as it is poisonous.

In many recipes in those days, they used limonette zest or juice, instead of the lemon we use today. Sweet Lime, (limonette, sometimes called bergamots) belongs to a diverse group of citrus hybrids that contain low acid pulp and juice, with less citron percentage. Obviously, it was common in central Europe, probably imported from Morocco.

Grandmother Ilona Binetter (Adler), 1906

2

Cream Cakes

I am still in the process of trying more and more of the many cream cakes in the recipe notebook. So far, I have decided to include the list below - the six most typically Austro-Hungarian desserts.

Dobos Tort
Cream Cake
Ladies' Whim
Madeira Sponge Cake
Indiáner
Chestnut Cream

The creams are based either on butter, egg whites or whipping cream. Each needs some skill to make it right. Most cakes come with their own specific cream and filling. For some recipes we added instructions for a chocolate ganache topping as the original had no specific cream included and we felt it to be necessary. In another cake we recommended a custard cream to replace a really complicated cream.

My recipe for **Chocolate Ganache:**
> 150 ml whipping cream
> 150g dark chocolate (ground)

Heat the whipping cream (almost boiling) and pour over the ground chocolate and mix until smooth.

The recipe notebook also includes creams to fill or cover any cake. The Raw Cream below is very good and easy.

Raw Cream for cake (Böske) Notebook page 3

3 egg yolks and one egg white, 4 large spoons to mix with powdered sugar, 160g butter, two bars of chocolate, 1 teaspoon of rum and mix for a very long time. Separately mix the butter with half the sugar and the other half with the eggs.

Ingredients:
- 3 egg yolks + 1 egg white
- 4 large tablespoons of confectioner sugar
- 140g of chocolate
- 160g butter
- 1 teaspoon rum

Raw Cream
JG

Instructions:

1. Mix the eggs with half of the sugar for a long time
2. Mix the butter with the other half of the sugar
3. Combine the two and add the chocolate and rum
4. Stir until completely smooth

PASTRIES FROM THE PAST - 15

Karlbader Oblate
JG

Special creams for the popular **Pischinger Cakes** on notebook pages 56 and 75, using *Karlsbader* waffles.

The *Karlsbader Oblaten* are a crispy round waffle specialty, with a fountain engraved on each. The waffles are freshly made by small bakers and sold on the streets of Prague. Originating from Bohemia, their spread came from the SPA triangle around Karlsbad (*Karlovy Vary*), to which they owe their name. Originally the Pischinger Torte was invented in Vienna, by Oskar Pischinger in the 1880s, a kind of a layer cake made from waffles and buttery, usually chocolate filling that became a sales success – a product that is now famous all over the world, especially in Europe.

Cream for Pischinger Cake (Notebook page 56)

150g sugar is boiled quite thick, 150g butter is stirred until fluffy, when the sugar has already cooled down, you add the same by spoonful to the butter while stirring constantly, when even colder stir it in 100g chocolate, which was boiled with a little water, finally you add it 1 handful of blanched hazelnuts, which have to be ground and strained first, and 8 *Karlsbader* waffles are filled with this and covered with chocolate icing.

Cream for Pischinger Cake (Notebook page 75)

120g butter, 120g sugar, stir it well, mix in 3 bars of chocolate, melted, 150g boiled and grated almonds then add two egg yolks. Spread on the waffles so that there is enough for the top.

Waffle Filling (Notebook page 18)

140g butter, 3 bars of dissolved chocolate, a little vanilla sugar to taste, 20-30 blanched crushed almonds, stir everything.

Dobos Torte

Notebook page 49
IB

Dobos Tort B

21 dka Zucker wird mit 8 Dotter und einem Stückchen Vanille flaumig gerührt, dann von 8 Eiklar den Schnee, nebst 12 dka Mehl leicht daruntergemischt. Fon diesem werden 8 Blätter gebacken; 28 dka Zucker wird mit 6 ganzen Eiern im Schnee Kessel auf sie die Wässer unter beständigem Schlagen der Schneeruthe so lange gelassen, bis dies zu einer dicken creme wird, dann wegstellen, ein Stückchen Vanille und 4 Zelteln Chocolade in die Creme reiben, wenn selbe schon lau ist, dann vermengt man dies mit 42 dka flaumig gerührter Tee Butter, so lange rührt man dies, bis es ganz kalt wird, dann werden die Blätter damit gefüllt, aufeinander gesetzt, die oberste Platte mit Salse dünn ausstreichen und mit 20 dka gebräuntem Zucker übergießen

Dobos Torte B (Notebook page 49)

210g sugar is stirred together with 8 yolks and a piece of vanilla until fluffy, then add the foam of 8 egg whites, along with 120g flour, lightly mixed in. From these bake 8 sheets. Cream: 280g sugar is mixed with 6 whole eggs in the a bowl over steam while constantly beating the whisk until it becomes a thick cream, then put away, grate a piece of vanilla and 4 bars of chocolate into the cream, if it is already lukewarm, then mix this with 420g fluffy tea butter, stir this until it gets really cold, then fill the sheets with it, put them on top of each other, spread the top plate thinly with marmalade and pour over 200g browned sugar.

Ingredients
Cake
6 eggs
100g granulated sugar
100g flour (all purpose)
1 tsp vanilla extract
Filling
125g confectioners' sugar
4 eggs
200g dark chocolate
250g butter (soft)
1 tsp vanilla extract
100g granulated sugar for the caramel crust

Instructions

1. Mix 100g sugar with 6 egg yolks and the vanilla until fluffy
2. Beat 6 egg whites and fold together with the yolks
3. Slowly mix 100g flour
4. Spread batter in 2 baking sheets of 10"x15" (25cm x 38cm), lined with parchment paper
5. Bake in 350°F (180°C) oven for 15 minutes. Let them cool and cut to 5" (12 cm) strips (for the 6 layers)

Niv in Vienna having Dobos Torte
Noga

The Filling

1. Mix confectioners' sugar with 4 whole eggs over a steam bowl to heat until 150°F (70°C), while whisking constantly. Remove from heat and keep whipping until cold (10 minutes) and becomes a thick cream
2. Whip the softened butter until creamy, add the melted chocolate and keep whipping until fluffy
3. Carefully combine the egg mixture into the chocolate. Refrigerate for 20 minutes
4. Fill the cream between the strips and lay them on top of each other and on the top of the 5th strip

Dobos Torte
Noga

The torte with the crust
JG

The crust

1. On the 6th strip, before laying it on the top of the torte, spread a thin layer of apricot jam
2. For the caramel crust melt 100g sugar until golden brown and pour over the 6th layer.
3. Cut into slices, with a sharp, buttered knife, before the caramel is completely cold and arrange them on the top of the torte

Dobos Torte is the most famous Hungarian cake, a 6 layers sponge cake with chocolate buttercream between the layers and topped with a layer of caramel. It was invented by József Carl Dobos (1847 - 1924), a Hungarian confectioner, chef and writer. He first introduced his famous cake, The Dobos Cake, at the National Exhibition in 1885, where the Emperor Franz Joseph I and Empress Elisabeth were among the first to taste it.

Both the chocolate buttercream and the dough were Dobos' invention. During his lifetime, the cake was often imitated, but never successfully reproduced.

Dobos Cake
JG

Dobos traveled to other countries in Europe to introduce his cake, and soon began exporting the product in specially designed wooden boxes. Near the end of his career, in 1906, Dobos donated his recipe to the Pastry and HoneycakeMakers' Guild (*Fővárosi Cukrász és Mézeskalácsos Ipartestület*).

Cream Cake

Notebook page 24
IB

Crem Torte

14deka Zucker, 5 Dotter etwas Zitronensaft mit schale sehr flaumig rühren, 8 Deka Reismehl, 5 Weisz Schnee kühl backen, wenn selbe kalt mit folgenden crem füllen: Crem – ¼ Liter süße Obers mit 3 Dotter, Stückchen Vanille in Schneekessel am Dunst schlagen dann schlagen, bis es kalt ist. 10deka Butter mit 12deka Vanillezucker sehr flaumig rühren, dann in die crem hineinrühren, die Torte durchschneiden und füllen.

Cream Cake (Notebook page 24)

Mix 140g sugar, 5 egg yolks, stir in a little lemon juice with the zest until very fluffy. Add 80g rice flour, 5 egg whites beaten to foam. Now bake low heat when its cold fill with the following cream:

Cream - Beat 250 ml of whipping cream with 3 yolks, a pinch of vanilla in the bowl over steam, then beat until it is cold. Mix 100g butter with 120g vanilla sugar until fluffy, then stir into the cream, cut through the cake and fill it.

The **Cream Cake** has a very special cake batter from rice meal that turned out surprisingly delicious, light and airy. The filling is very similar to a French Butter Cream, quite difficult to make and can be substituted with custard cream or an alternative Vanilla Pastry Cream.

Ingredients

   5 eggs
   100g granulated sugar
   80g rice flour
   1 lemon juice and zest

Filling

   100ml whipping cream
   3 egg yolks
   ½ tsp vanilla
   50g confectioners' sugar
   100g butter (soft)

Instructions

1. Mix the sugar with the egg yolks
2. Stir in a little lemon juice and the zest
3. Stir until fluffy then add the rice flour
4. Beat the egg whites to a stiff foam and fold into the batter
5. Pour into a parchment paper lined square baking pan of 10" (25cm)
6. Bake in a preheated oven of 325°F (160°C), about 35 minutes and let it cool

The Filling

1. Whip the butter with the confectioners' sugar until fluffy, make sure it is not too soft (refrigerate for 10 minutes, if needed)
2. Beat the whipping cream with the yolks and vanilla over a steam bowl (bain marie) until it becomes thick (can take 10 minutes)

Cream Cake
JG

3. Remove from heat and keep beating until it is gets to room temperature (about 10 minutes)
4. Add slowly, a spoon at a time of the butter into the egg mixture while stirring
5. Whip the resulting cream to a fluffy light cream
6. Cut the cake in two equal parts for layers and fill the cream between, make sure you have enough cream to cover and decorate the top
7. Refrigerate for a couple of hours before serving

Cream Cake slice
JG

Bain Marie
JG

When baking or cooking you will often encounter the term **"Bain Marie"**. It is in French *bain de Marie* or *bain-marie*, a double boiler or hot water bath (Mary's bath), used for cooking delicate foods, over low temperatures, by using the steam the Bain Marie creates. This is useful to make temperamental creams and sauces like Hollandaise and egg-based creams, custards or gently melting things like butter or chocolate.

It is a saucepan with high sides, and a heat proof bowl to fit onto the top of the saucepan. To create the steam the saucepan, with about 4 inches of water, is heated on the stove so that the bowl does not touch the simmering water in the saucepan.

The butter cream
JG

Ladies' Whim

Damen Capricen

14dka Butter wird mit 14dka Mehl gut abgebröselt, 10dka Zucker und 10dkg Haselnüsse, welche in der Röhre etwas geröstet würden, gemahlen, dies alles gut vermischen, mit 1 Eidotter eingeknetet, auf den blech dünn ausgewalkt, mit Himbeere Salse dünn aufgestrichen und bei gelinder Hitze schön rosa gebacken. Dann wird von 7 Eiklar der Schnee mit 21dka Vanillezucker vermengt, darauf gestrichen, bei geher Hitze rosa gebacken, auf dem Blech in Vierecke geschnitten, auf die Schüssel gelegt und als kalter serviert.

Ladies' Whim (Notebook page 45)

140g butter is crumbled well with 140g flour, 100g sugar and 100g ground hazelnuts roasted a little in the oven, mix all this well, knead with 1 egg yolk, roll out thinly on a baking sheet, spread thinly with raspberry marmalade and bake pink over a gentle heat. Beat 7 egg whites mixed with 210g vanilla sugar to a foam, spread on top, bake pink over high heat, cut into squares on the tray, placed in a bowl and served cold.

Notebook page 45
IB

Ingredients

- 140g butter (soft)
- 140g flour (all purpose)
- 80g sugar
- 100g hazelnuts (roasted and ground)
- 1 egg yolk
- 3 egg whites
- 80g confectioners' sugar
- 1 tsp vanilla extract
- 2/3 cup raspberry jam

Instructions

1. Mix butter, flour, sugar and nuts until becomes crumbly, add 1 egg yolk, and knead to a ball
2. Roll out into a 9 x 9" (22 x 22cm) baking pan lined with parchment paper bake in a preheated oven of 350F° (180C°) for 15-20 minutes until golden brown.
3. Remove from oven and let it cool slightly then spread on raspberry jam
4. Beat 3 egg whites with vanilla until it forms peaks, add the confectioners' sugar, beat until stiff and shiny
5. Spoon the beaten egg whites on top of the cake and bake again in 375°F (190°C) oven until lightly brown, about 15 minutes
6. Cut into squares with a sharp knife

Ladies' Whim
JG

Ladies' Whim is an old Hungarian recipe "*női szeszély*", which was very popular decades ago. In the recipe notebook I have a few versions. It was and is also popular all-around eastern Europe with names like "*damin kapric*" or "*damin ćef*" or "*damina nature*".

Ladies' Whim layers
JG

Ladies' Whim
JG

The origin of the name is unknown, but the different versions that float around may suggest that the ingredients women used to make this cake depended on their actual (whimsical) mood. The most varied part of this pastry is the base, some recipes call for a yeasted dough, others make it with a sponge batter.

Madeira Cream Sponge Cake

Notebook page 12
IB

Biskuit Torte mit Madeira fülle
14deka Zucker mit 6 Dotter flaumig abtrieben, 3 Ei klare Schnee und langsam resp nach und nach 10deka Mehl feineinrühren, langsam backen.

Fülle hiezu
4 Dotter, 7deka Zucker, 4 Löffel Madeira, werden kochende zu rinnen dicken crem geschlagen. Man schlägt ihn dann bis er kalt wird, rührt 1 Deziliter (¼ Seidl) Schlagobers hinein, füllt damit die ausgehöhlte torte, auf die man wieder den Deckel gibt, oder macht es in anderer Form schneidet das Biskuit in Scheiben, die man abwechselnd mit crem legt – der Zwieback ist sehr schön, nicht als torte sondern in länghinen Model gebacken, zu dienen Scheiben geschnitten und immer eine Reihe Biskuit, eine crem und so weiter. Die Madeira von welchen eine Flasche sich lange erhalt, kauft man unter den Namen Hochmadeira.

Sponge Cake with Madeira Fill (Notebook page 12)
Mix 140g sugar with 6 yolks until fluffy, beat 3 eggs whites to foam and slowly or gradually stir in 100g flour, bake slowly.

The Fill
4 yolks, 70g sugar, 4 spoons of Madeira are whipped into a thick cream while cooking. You then beat it until it gets cold, stir in 100 ml (¼ Seidl) whipping cream, fill the hollowed-out cake with it and put the lid back on, or make another form, cut the cake into slices, which you put alternately with cream - the rusk is very nice, not as a cake but baked in a lengthwise baking tray, to serve, slice and always a row of biscuit, a row of cream and so on. Madeira, from which a bottle lasts for a long time, is bought under the name *Hochmadeira*.

Ingredients

6 egg yolks
3 egg whites
140g granulated sugar
100g flour

Filling

4 egg yolks
50g confectioners' sugar
4 tbs Madeira wine
150g butter (soft)

Madeira Cream Sponge Cake
JG

Madeira Cream Cake, rectangle version
JG

Instructions

1. Beat 3 egg whites and set aside
2. Mix sugar with 6 egg yolks until fluffy
3. Fold the egg whites into the egg yolks
4. Slowly stir in the flour
5. Pour into a parchment lined, square 10" x 10" baking pan or 2 round 8" (20 cm) baking pans
6. Bake in a preheated oven of 360°F (160°C) for 25 – 30 minutes

The Filling

1. Stir the softened butter until creamy and set aside
2. Stir 4 egg yolks with the confectioners' sugar over steam bowl
3. Add 4 tbs Madeira wine and keep whisking until it becomes a thick cream. Remove from heat and keep beating until it gets cold
4. Add the butter to the eggs, spoon by spoon, while whipping
5. Cut the square sponge cake into two equal parts for layers or use the 2 round cakes and fill the cream between the layers and on the top

Madeira cream steam bowl
JG

Madeira wine
JG

The rugged Portuguese island of Madeira is right off the coast of Morocco features steep vineyards planted in volcanic soils. It was an important port during the 1400s and 1500s, when sailors would stop there for trading and supplies, including the local wine.

Exposed to hot sun on the open seas, however, the wine would often spoil. So, its makers took a cue from Porto producers and fortified the stuff with a sugar distillate to ensure its survival through the course of the voyage. Sailors soon discovered that the longer that Madeira sat on their ships, the deeper its flavor became.

Today, the wine is fortified with brandy and it is exposed to heat and oxygen while aging at the vineyard.

"The beautiful thing about Madeira is, even though i's a fortified wine, styles range anywhere from bone dry to intensely sweet," says Sam Gamble, head sommelier of Atlas restaurant in Atlanta and "There are no bad bottles."[1]

1. Lia Picard, (2020, August 20), How Madeira Transformed to a Fortified Powerhouse, WhineEnthusiast, https://www.winemag.com/2020/08/20/madeira-fortified-wine/

Indiáner

Notebook page 5
IB

Indianer Torte
Zu 5 ganze Eier 12deka Zucker, 6deka Mehl in Schnee Kessel unter fortwährendem rühren zu kochen gegeben, zu allerletzte kommen die 6deka Mehl verrührt. Wenn die Torte fertig ist, 2 geschnitten, ein wenig ausgehöhlt und mit Schlagobers gefüllt oben eine Chocolade Glasur.

Indiáner Cake (Notebook page 5)
To 5 whole eggs add 120g sugar, 60g flour in a bowl over heat while stirring continuously, at the very last mix 60g more flour. When the cake is ready, cut in two, hollow it out a little and fill it with whipped cream on top a chocolate glaze.

Indiáner mit Schlagobers
JG

Ingredients

Dough

5 eggs
120g granulated sugar
120g flour (all purpose)

Chocolate Ganache

150ml whipping cream
150g dark chocolate (ground)

Cream

400ml whipping cream
50g confectioners' sugar

Instructions

1. Stir the whole eggs with the granulated sugar in a steam bowl until fluffy
2. Add half the flour and whip continuously until light and creamy
3. Add the rest of the flour and keep stirring
4. Pour the dough into very shallow cookie baking form, lightly buttered (about 16 pieces)
5. Bake in a 350°F (180°C) oven for 25 minutes or until lightly brown. Let them cool
6. Prepare the chocolate ganache from the whipping cream and dark chocolate
7. Dip the bottom of each cookie into the chocolate ganache. Let them cool and harden

Indianer
JG

The cream

1. Beat the whipping cream with the confectioner sugar until stiff
2. Fill cream between 2 coated cookies

The origin of the **Indiáner** cake is linked to the Theater an der Wien, when it was owned and administered by Count Ferdinánd Pálffy von Erdöd, between 1807 and 1826. who purchased the theater in 1813. During its management, which lasted until 1826, he staged operas, ballets and for the first time in Vienna, pantomime and variety, losing a lot of money in elaborate shows that forced him to sell the theater at auction in 1826.[1]

Theater an der Wien (c. 1800)
Schloß Schönbrunn Kultur- und Betriebsges.m.b.H./Foto: Julia Teresa Friehs

While the theater was failing, Count Pálffy learned that an Indian-born artist was touring Europe and captivating audiences everywhere with his wonderful stunts. He contacted the Indian artist's impresario and managed to contract him to perform in Vienna. To celebrate this the Count assigned his chef to invent some sweets, for the evening of the first performance, to be similar in color to the Indian artist's skin. They served this novelty to each theater visitor upon entry for free. The audience liked it very much, even more than the artist on stage. The next day, the whole of Vienna rushed to the bakeshops and looked for the new Indiáner cake.

The Theater exist to this day and the indiáner cake has been around for more than two hundred years and was still a favorite of children when I was growing up in Budapest.

1. (n.d.). *Theater an der Wien*. Histouring. https://www.histouring.com/en/historical-places/theater-an-der-wien/

Chestnut Cream

Notebook page 9
IB

Kastanien Creme

½ kg Kastanien wird roh geschält, dann in Milch weich gesotten und durch ein feines Sieb passiert; dann wird ½ Liter süßer Rahm mit einem Stückchen Vanille und Zucker gekocht, an 8 verrührte Eigelb gerührt, ein wenigen stehen lassen und zuletzt die passierten Kastanien auf dem Feuer daran rühren 40 Gram aufgelöste Gelatine darunter mengen und wenn es erkaltet ist, ein starkes ½ Liter Schlagrahm hineinmengen, etwas Maraschino und ein Handvoll Sultaninen ebenfalls mit der Masse vermengt und dann auf die Schüssel gegeben.

Chestnut Cream (Notebook page 9)

½ kg chestnuts are peeled raw, then boiled in milk until soft and strained through a fine sieve; Then ½ liter of sweet cream is boiled with a piece of vanilla and sugar, mix in 8 stirred egg yolks, let stand a little and finally stir in the chestnuts while on heat, add 40 grams of dissolved gelatin and when it is cold, add a strong ½ liter whipped cream, add some maraschino and a handful of sultanas to the mixture and then pour into a bowl.

Ingredients

- 440g chestnut* mashed
- 500ml whipping cream
- 7 egg yolks
- 50g granulated sugar
- 50g raisins (sultana)
- 1/2tbs vanilla extract
- 2tbs maraschino liquor (or Rum)
- 15g Gelatine (1 pouch, unflavoured)
- Whipping cream to top

* I am using 1 can of unsweetened chestnut puree of 439g, by Clement Faugier

Chestnut Cream in the fridge
JG

Instructions

1. Boil the whipping cream in a saucepan with sugar and vanilla
2. Whisk the egg yolks in a bowl. Take the saucepan off the heat and mix in the yolk.
3. Let the mixture stand for a while – 30 minutes, to let it thicken
4. Heat up the saucepan and mix in the chestnuts, while heating
5. Dissolve the gelatin (as instructed on the packaging) and mix in
6. Add the maraschino and the raisins and stir well
7. Pour the mixture into small bowls and refrigerate
8. When the cream is cold and solidified top with stiffly beaten whipping crem (sweetened or unsweetened, as you like)

Chestnut Cream
JG

The Chestnut Cream is a variation on the **Chestnut Purée,** which is a very popular dessert in Hungary and a nostalgic favorite from my childhood.

Chestnut Purée
JG

The Chestnut Purée is a dessert of sweetened chestnut purée in the form of vermicelli, topped with whipped cream, originating in France, called *Mont Blanc* as the huge pile of whipped cream resembles that snow-capped mountain. A dish called *entremets du Mont-Blanc*, described as a sweet combination of chestnuts and cream, invented by the Dessat(s) pastry-shop approximately around 1847.

However, there are claims that *Mont Blanc* is a copy of the Italian *Monte Bianco*. *Monte Bianco's* recipe already appeared in a cookbook printed in Florence in 1475. And that later it was a common dessert on Cesare and Lucrezia Borgia's table. It appeared in France only around 1620.

3

Nut Cakes

In my grandmother's recipe book, there are a surprisingly large number of cake recipes made exclusively with different kinds of nuts. No wheat flour or breadcrumbs added. I was surprised to learn that baking gluten free cakes was already so popular in the early 20th century. I wonder how this abundance of nut cakes was related to health consciousness or just the availability of nut flour versus wheat flour. Chestnuts seems to be very popular cake ingredient in Austria and Hungary. The chestnut cream was my favorite childhood dessert.

Nuts have many dietary benefits. A wealth of data from health research, diet studies and clinical trials suggest that nuts are highly nutritious, contain important vitamins, protein, unsaturated fats, fibers and minerals, while low in carbohydrates.

Nuts
JG

Different types of nuts have slight differences in their vitamin and mineral content. For example, among the vitamins and minerals, raw chestnuts contain are vitamin B1, B2, B6, vitamin C, vitamin E, potassium, magnesium, iron, copper, and phosphorus.

I collected some of those recipes in this section for each type of nut used – almonds, hazelnuts, walnuts and chestnuts. You will find even that a couple of cakes which use two type of nuts like the Snow Cake.

Most of the recipes specifically instruct to lightly roast the nuts before grinding them. Almonds and hazelnuts most of the time, but roasting walnuts is never recommended in my grandmother's recipe notebook. I became curios about this and found research on the subject that indicates that roasting nuts in high temperature create a chemical change that affects their composition and health benefits, while improves their taste and texture. The recommendation is to roast nuts at medium temperature of 250°F - 265°F (120°C – 160°C).

Roasting almonds in the oven
JG

Before grinding nuts, make sure they are completely cold. How fine to grind/grate or crush them and how to mix into the batter varies according to recipe. Some recipes ask for almonds with the skin or blanched or clean hazelnuts from most of their skin. My expert friend, Leora, insists that roasting and griding the nuts yourself, as opposed to store bought nuts meal, has a big impact on the quality of the resulting cake. Also, you have control over how fine the ground nuts are – just crushed, grinded or finely grinded.

Nuts are also used extensively for texture and decoration – slivered or sliced almonds, candied chestnuts, whole or crumbled hazelnuts or walnuts.

See the recipes is this section:

Stefania Cake
Chestnut Cake
Sacher Torte - Chocolate Icing
Maraschino Walnut Cake
Snow Cake
Walnut Cream Cake

Nut Cakes
JG

Stefánia Cake

Notebook page 20
IB

Stefánia Torta

8 tojásfehérjének a habjához 25 deka cukrot és 25 deka őrölt hámozott mogyorót keverünk és két részben sütjük. Töltelék: 8 tojássárgája, 15 deka cukor, egy rúd vanília és 5-6 evőkanál tejet fel forralunk és ha kissé sűrűsödni kezd 4 tábla puhított csokoládét keverünk hozzá. Ha kehült, 6 deka vajat teszünk apránként bele és töltjük a tortát. Felül hámozott mogyoróval díszítjük.

Stefánia Cake (Notebook page 20)

To 8 beaten egg whites, mix 250g sugar and 250g ground, peeled hazelnuts and bake in two parts. Filling: 8 egg yolks, 150g sugar, a stick of vanilla and 5-6 tablespoons of milk to boil and when it starts to thicken a little, add 150g of softened chocolate. Once cool, add 60g butter little by little and fill the cake. Garnish with peeled hazelnuts on top.

Ingredients

    8 eggs whites
    150g granulated sugar
    250g hazelnuts (ground)

Filling

    8 egg yolks
    150g dark chocolate
    1 tsp vanilla extract
    100g confectioners' sugar
    5-6 tablespoons milk
    60g butter

Instructions

1. Roast hazelnuts lightly 10-15 minutes in a 250°F (120°C) oven. Peel by rubbing in a clean tea towel or colander. Grind in a food processor
2. Beat the egg whites until forms soft peaks, add the sugar and mix until dissolved. Add the peeled, ground hazelnuts
3. Spread the batter on two rectangular baking sheets 10"x 15" (25cm x 38cm), lined with parchment paper in preheated oven, 350°F (180°C) for 25-30 minutes
4. Cut to 5" (12cm) strips (for the 6 layers)

Stefánia Cake (with Maya)
JG

The Filling

1. Beat the egg yolks with the sugar and vanilla over a steam bowl until thick (10 minutes)
2. Heat 5-6 tablespoons of milk to add to the melted chocolate. Add the butter little by little
3. Mix the egg yolks and chocolate lightly. If the cream is not thick enough, refrigerate for an hour
1. Spread the filling between each layer and dust the top layer with cocoa powder

Stefánia Cake is a Dobos Torte without the caramel, as my aunt Klári told me.

Stefánia cake can be filled with chocolate buttercream or chocolate ganache, and the top dusted with raw cocoa powder. Stefánia has one more layer than the Dobos, making it a seven layer cake. To support 7 layers of cream, Stefánia has to have stable cake layers. In our version it is made of 6 layers of finely ground hazelnuts, instead of flour. The cake is best when it is thoroughly chilled.

Stefánia Cake
JG

The Eastern European patisserie calls both the Polish "*Ciasto Stefanka*" and the Hungarian "*Stefánia Torta*" by the name "Seven Sisters". The seven sisters refer to its seven layers (six layers in most Hungarian versions).

Chestnut Cake

Notebook page 29
IB

Gesztenye Torta

21dka áttört gesztenyét, 28dka cukorral és 8 tojássárgájával pelyhesen kavarunk, ebbe 8 tojásfehérjéből készült sűrű habot, kis vaníliát, 3 ½ dka lisztet és végül 10 ½ felolvasztott vajat lassan egymásután belekavarunk. Ezen tömeget kétlapban megsütjük. Most 7dka megfőtt és áttört gesztenyéből ½ messely tejhabból, 7dka cukorból és kis vaníliából tölteléket készítünk. Végül a tortát kávé konzervvel bevonjuk és kis csokoládé gesztenyével díszítjük.

Chestnut Cake (Notebook page 29)

Stir until fluffy 210g mashed chestnuts, 280g sugar and 8 egg yolks, mix in slowly dense foam from 8 egg whites, add little vanilla, then 35gram flour and finally 105g melted butter. Bake this mixture in two sheets. Now we make a filling from 70g boiled and mashed chestnuts 2/5-liter whipping cream, 70gram sugar and a little vanilla. Finally, the cake is coated with canned coffee and garnished with small chocolate chestnuts.

Ingredients

Cake

330g chestnuts* (mashed)
210g granulated sugar
70g almond meal or flour
8 eggs
1 tsp vanilla extract
105g butter (melted)

Filling

110 mashed chestnuts
400ml whipping cream
70g granulated sugar
1 tsp vanilla extract

*I am using 1 can of unsweetened chestnut puree of 439g, by Clement Faugier

Instructions

1. Beat the egg yolks with the sugar until fluffy
2. Mix in lightly the mashed chestnuts
3. Beat the egg whites into a stiff foam
4. Fold in the egg whites
5. Add 1 tsp vanilla extract
6. Mix in almond meal or flour
7. Stir in the melted butter
8. Pour into a square, well greased baking sheets
9. Bake in a preheated oven 350°F (180°C) for 45 – 50 minutes

Chestnut Cake
JG

Chestnut Cake
JG

The Filling

1. Make a strong foam from the whipping cream and sugar
2. Add the mashed chestnuts and vanilla extract
3. Cut the square cake into two equal parts for the layers
4. Fill between the layers and coat over the cake
5. Decorate with coffee syrup and/or candied chestnuts

Chestnuts are very popular in Hungary, mainly used for delicious cakes and desserts. Some types are toxic and shouldn't be eaten.

Chestnuts
Erin Lizotte (left) and Virginia Rinkel (center and right).

Left - Edible chestnut with spiny husk and pointed tassel on tip.
Center - Fleshy husk of horse chestnut
Right - Rounded toxic horse chestnuts without a tassel

Before boiling chestnut in the shell, it is important to know that after peeling off the shell for 700g chestnut in shell you will have 450g shelled chestnuts. How to boil chestnuts:

- Bring a pot of water to boil
- Cut an X into the shell of each chestnut with a sharp knife
- Boil them for 5-10 minutes, Drain and let them cool
- Peel the shell and skin

Sacher Torte
Chocolate Icing

Notebook page 7
IB

Sacher Torte
14 Deka Zucker flaumig mit 8 Dotter abtreiben, 14 Deka Mandeln, 16 Deka Chocolade, 10 Bohnen geriebenen Kaffee, 1 Orangensaft samt Schale, 3 Deka Butter, 3 Deka Brösel, 6 Schnee mit Chocolade beeisen.

Sacher Torte (Notebook page 7)
Mix 140g sugar with 8 yolks until fluffy. Add 140g almond flour, 160g Chocolate, 10 grated coffee beans, 1 orange juice with the zest, 30g butter, and 30g crumbs, 6 egg whites beaten to foam. Cover with chocolate icing.

Ingredients
Cake
100g granulated sugar

8 eggs

140g almond (lightly roasted, finely ground)

160g dark chocolate (melted)

1 shot coffee (strong)

1 orange zest

Juice from half orange

30g butter (melted)

30g rice flour (or breadcrumbs)

1/3 cup apricot jam

Sacher Torte
JG

Instructions

1. Mix sugar with yolks until fluffy
2. Add melted chocolate, coffee, orange juice and zest, melted butter, rice flour and lastly ground almonds
3. Beat the egg whites to a stiff foam
4. Mix the foam lightly into the chocolate batter
5. Bake in a moderate 350°F (180°C) oven in a 10" (26cm) greased baking form for 45 minutes
6. Let the cake cool and cover with a thin layer of apricot jam

Notebook page 53
IB

Chocolade Überguss zu Torten
Man mischt zu 3 Zelteln Chocolade zweimal so schwer Zucker, die Chocolade wird früher in der Röhre gewärmt, der Zucker wird mit 2 Obers Löffel Wasser befeuchtet und so lang gekocht bis es schwere Tropfen wirst, dann gießt man selben löffelweise in die gewärmte Chocolade unter beständigem umrühren; Wenn dies schon so ziemlich ausgekühlt ist, triebt man ein nussgroses Stück Butter dazwischen und rührt es solange bis die Glasur ganz auskühlt. Überziehe nun die dazu bestimmte Torte damit und verziere sie mit Obst.

Chocolate icing (Notebook page 53)
Mix twice as heavy sugar into 3 bars of chocolate, the chocolate is first warmed in the oven, the sugar is moistened with 2 (cream) spoons of water and cooked until it becomes heavy drops, then pour it by spoonful into the warmed chocolate under constant stir; When this is pretty much cooled, you mix a nut-sized piece of butter in between and stir it until the glaze has cooled completely. Now cover the intended cake with it and decorate it with fruit.

Ingredients

Icing

150g dark chocolate

75g confectioners' sugar

30g butter

2 tbs water

Instructions

1. Melt the chocolate
2. Cook the sugar with a little water until it becomes thick
3. Drip the sugar into the chocolate spoon by spoon and keep stirring
4. When lukewarm stir in 30g butter and keep stirring until cold
5. Cover the cake

Sacher Torte
JG

Sacher Torte
JG

Sacher Torte is a very famous Viennese delicacy - dark chocolate sponge cake with apricot jam and a thin layer of bittersweet chocolate icing. While the original recipe is using flour, this version from my grandmother's recipes is with almond flour. This is how I remember it from my childhood.

The Sacher Torte was a closely guarded secret recipe from 1832 created by young Franz Sacher, apprentice at the court of Prince Metternich, the State Chancellor. The story goes that he was given the order to create a dessert for guests of the court, to rescue the evening when the chef was off sick one day. The guests were very pleased with the cake created by Sacher.

Sacher Torte slice
JG

After Sacher completed his training as a chef, he opened a specialty delicatessen and wine shop in his hometown of Vienna. His eldest son, Eduard carried on his culinary legacy.

Eduard completed his training in Vienna with the Royal and Imperial pastry Chef at the Demel Bakery and Chocolatier. At this time, Eduard improved his father's recipe and developed the cake into its current form today which was first served at the Demel and later at the Hotel Sacher founded by Eduard in 1876.

Since then, the cake remains among the most well known culinary specialties of Vienna.

Maraschino Walnut Cake

Notebook page 78
IB

Nuss Torte 2
20dka Zucker mit 6 Dottern gut abtrieben, 5dka geriebene Chocolade, 20dka geriebene Nüsse und zuletzt mit Maraschino befürchte Semmelbrösel hinein. Den Schnee von 6 Klar leicht verrühren. Die Masse mit Butter bestrichene form backen lassen.

Nut cake 2 (Notebook page 78)
Mix 200g sugar with 6 yolks, add 50g grated chocolate, 200g grated walnuts and finally breadcrumbs scented with Maraschino. Gently stir in the beaten foam from 6 egg whites. Bake the mixture in a buttered form.

Maraschino Walnut Cake slice
JG

Ingredients

- 150g granulated sugar
- 6 eggs
- 50g dark chocolate (grated)
- 200g walnuts (ground)
- 4 tbs breadcrumbs
- 5 tbs Maraschino or other liquor

Maraschino Walnut Cake
JG

Instructions

1. Beat the egg whites with 2 tbs sugar until stiff
2. Mix breadcrumbs and liquor
3. Beat egg yolks with remaining sugar until fluffy. Add breadcrumbs, walnuts and chocolate.
4. Fold in the egg whites gradually
5. Bake in a greased baking form in 350°F (180°C) oven for 45 minutes
6. Can be topped with chocolate ganache

> Maraschino is a liqueur obtained from the distilled Marasca cherries. The small, slightly sour fruit of the Tapiwa cherry tree, which grows wild along parts of the Dalmatian coast, lends the liqueur its unique aroma.

Maraschino Liquor
JG

Snow Cake

Notebook page 18
IB

Schnee Torte
Von 7 Ei klar Schnee, 10dka Nüsse, 10dka Mandeln, 17dka gestoßenen Zucker Vanille Geruch, Zitronen schalle. Bei mäßigem Feuer backen.

Snow Cake (Notebook page 18)
From 7 egg whites beat to foam, add 100g walnuts, 100g almonds, 170g crushed sugar - vanilla smell, lemon zest. Bake on a moderate heat.

Ingredients
7 egg whites
80g granulated sugar
100g walnuts (ground)
100g almonds (ground)
1 tsp vanilla extract
1 lemon zest

Snow Cake
JG

Instructions
1. Beat the egg whites to a stiff foam
2. Add the sugar, vanilla and lemon zest
3. Slowly add walnuts and almonds and mix well
4. Pour the batter into a well greased baking form
5. Bake in a preheated oven 350°F (180°C) for 45 minutes

Snow Cake with Madeira cream
JG

Walnut Cream Cake

Notebook page 7
IB

Nuss Torte

16dka Zucker mit 6 Eidotter ½ Stunde rühren, hernach 14dka fein gestoßene Nüsse gut hinein rühren, 1 Taferl fein geriebenen Chocolade, ein messerspitz gemahlen Kaffee und den Schnee von 6 Eiweiß, in die Tortenform geben ¾ stunden backen und wen selbe ausgekühlt entzweischneiden und mit folgender Fülle gefüllt.

Fülle: Schnee von 2 Ei klar, 8 dka Zucker, 1 Taferl hineingeriebene Chocolade, 1 Esslöffel fein gestoßene Nüsse hineinmischen. Die Torte damit füllt, ein paar Minuten noch in der Röhre lassen, mit Chocolade Glasur glasiert und mit halben Nüssen belegen.

Walnuts Cake (Notebook page 7)

Stir 160g sugar with 6 egg yolks for ½ hour, then stir in well 140g finely pounded walnuts, 1 bar of finely grated chocolate, a knife edge ground coffee, and the beaten foam of 6 egg whites, bake in the cake form for ¾ hours and then cut in half and fill with the following.

Filling: Beaten foam from 2 egg whites, 80g sugar, 1 bar of grated chocolate, mix in 1 tablespoon of finely pounded walnuts. Fill the cake with it, leave it in the oven for a few minutes, glaze it with chocolate glaze and top it with half nuts.

Ingredients

Cake
120 + 20g granulated sugar
6 eggs
140g + 1 tbs walnuts (finely ground)
50g dark chocolate (finely ground)
½ tsp coffee (ground)

Cream
50g dark chocolate (finely ground)
60g granulated sugar
2 egg whites

Icing
100g dark chocolate (melted)
20g confectioners' sugar
50g butter

Walnut Cream Cake slice
JG

Instructions

1. Beat 120g sugar and the egg yolks until fluffy. Mix in ground chocolate and coffee
2. Beat the the egg whites with 20g sugar until a stiff foam
3. Fold in lightly the egg whites with the yolks
4. Bake in a well greased square 10" x 10" (26cm) baking form in 350°F (180°C) oven for 45 minutes
5. Let the cake cool and cut into two equal parts for layers

The cream

1. Beat the egg whites until stiff
2. Mix into the foam the ground chocolate
3. Add 1 tbs ground walnuts
4. Spread the cream between the two layers and on top of the cake

Walnut Cream Cake with Icing
JG

The Icing

1. Boil sugar in a small amount of water until thick
2. Spoon the sugar liquid into the melted chocolate slowly and mix
3. Mix in the butter and keep stirring
4. Spread the chocolate Icing on top and sides of the cake
5. Decorate with half walnuts

4

Puddings

Puddings must have been a very popular dessert back then because the recipe notebook includes several recipes. They are called alternatively *"koch"*, *"shaum"* or *"pudding"*. They can be chocolate or rum-flavored, made of rice, almonds or hazelnuts, and they all have a lot of eggs - 6 to 8 eggs. They were very popular during the Christmas season.

Steam oven / water bath
JG

What gives the cake a consistency of pudding is the method of steam baking: A well-greased baking dish with the mixture is placed in a pan of boiling water in the oven and steamed in medium heat for a long time – 45 minutes to an hour. The best baking dish for puddings is a tube pan that allows the steam to reach the center, to have an evenly baked result.

Usually, puddings are served with chaudeau or fruit sauce. Chaudeau (*chaude eau* French for warm water), is a sweet wine foam, which originally only consists of egg yolk, sugar and white wine and is boiled in a water bath or steamed in a bain-marie.

Choosing the right wine is essential in the preparation, sparkling wine or champagne is particularly fine. A dash of cognac or sherry can be also nice. Alternatively, the Chaudeau can be prepared with red or rosé wine.

Red wine Chaudeau from recipe notebook page 13: 40ml red wine, 8 egg yolks, 160g sugar.

For **Fruit Sauce**, I like to prepare strawberry and rhubarb sauce:
- 4 cups diced strawberries
- 4 cups diced rhubarb
- 1 lemon juice
- 3 tbs sugar
- 3 tbs water

Combine the strawberries, rhubarb, lemon juice, sugar and water in a medium-sized saucepan. Bring it to a boil and let it cook on low heat for about 30-45 minutes, cook less or longer depending on how thick you want it.

Red Wine Chaudeau
JG

The recipes included in this section:
Almond Pudding
Hazelnut Pudding
Chocolate Cook
Chocolate Foam
Rice Pudding
Moor in Shirt

Almond Pudding

Notebook page 13
IB

Mandel Pudding

Man gibt 12deka gestoßenen Zucker, 12deka Mandeln zu rösten, bis sie gelb geworden, nehme man sie von Feuer fort, überlehre sie in ein anderes Gefäß und stoße sie gänzlichen erkälten sein, 16deka Zucker werden mit 8 Eidotter ¼ Stunde gerührt, die gestoßenen Mandeln dazugegeben und mit dem safte eine Zitrone und ein Gewürznelken ½ Stunde gerührt, worin man den Schnee von 8 Ei klar leicht einmischt. In eine Butter bestrichene mit Mehl bestreute Puddingform wird diese Maße gefüllt, welche dann man ¾ Stunden in Dunst kochen lasst, in eine Schüssel stürzt und mit Chaudeau zu Tisch gibt, 4deci roten Wein, 8 Eidotter, 16deka Zucker.

Almond Pudding (Notebook page 13)

Give 120g granulated sugar, roast 120g almonds until they turn yellow, take them away from the fire, transfer them to another bowl and crush them completely until they are completely cold, 160g sugar is stirred with 8 egg yolks for ¼ hour, the crushed almonds are added and stirred with the juice of a lemon and a clove for ½ hour, in which you mix foam from 8 egg whites. This mass is filled into a buttered pudding mold sprinkled with flour, which is then left to cook for ¾ hours in steam, poured into a bowl and served with Chaudeau, 40ml red wine, 8 egg yolks, 160g sugar.

Ingredients

- 60g + 60g + 20g granulated sugar
- 8 eggs
- 120g almonds (blanched, ground)
- ½ tbs cloves (ground)
- Juice from 1 lemon

Almond Pudding
JG

Instructions

Almond Pudding
JG

1. Roast the blanched almonds with 60g sugar until they are pink and let it cool completely before grinding them
2. Beat the egg yolks with 60g sugar until fluffy
3. Add almonds, then lemon juice and clove. Keep beating
4. Beat the egg whites to foam with 20g sugar
5. Mix everything together lightly
6. Bake in a moderate 350°F (180°C) oven in a greased baking dish placed in a pan of boiling water, for 55 min
7. Turn it over to a plate. Can be served with Chaudeau

Hazelnut Pudding

Notebook page 46
IB

Haselnuss Pudding

7 dka reis wird in etwas mehr als 2 Deziliter Milch gekocht und passiert, 10 dka Butter mit 8 Eidotter flaumig abgetrieben, 10 dka fein gestroßene Haselnüsse, 8 dka Zucker mit Vanille gestoßen und alles dies gut abtrieben. Nun vermengt man von 7 Ei klar den Schnee leicht dazu und backt dies ¾ Stunden in Dunst langsam, dann wird derselbe gestürzt und mit Fruchtsaft serviert.

Hazelnut Pudding (Notebook page 46)

70g rice is cooked in a little more than 200ml of milk and mashed, 100g butter with 8 egg yolks whipped until fluffy, 100g finely ground hazelnuts, 80g sugar crushed with vanilla and all this mixed well. Now you mix in the foam from 7 egg whites and bake it slowly in steam for ¾ hours, then turn it over and serve it with fruit sauce.

Ingredients

- 70g white rice
- 250ml milk
- 100g butter
- 7 eggs
- 80g + 20g granulated sugar
- 100g hazelnuts (roasted, finely ground)
- 1 tsp vanilla extract

Hazelnut Pudding
JG

Hazelnut Pudding with fruit sauce
JG

Instructions

1. Cook the rice in the milk until soft. Let it cool and then mash it
2. Add butter, 80g sugar and the egg yolks and whisk until fluffy
3. Add the hazelnuts and vanilla and mix completely
4. Beat the egg whites with 20g sugar to a stiff foam
5. Mix all together lightly
6. Steam in 350°F (180°C) oven in a well greased baking dish placed in a pan of boiling water for 55 minutes
7. Turn it over onto a plate. Serve with fruit sauce

Chocolate Cook

Notebook page 18
IB

Chocolade Koch
4 Eigelb, 4 Löffel Zucker gut abtreiben, 5dka ungeschälte Mandeln hiezu, 2 Löffel Semmelbrösel, 2 Taferl erweichte Chocolade mit verrührt, von klaren den Schnee, etwas Zitronensaft. Die Form mit fette und Brösel angeschmiert in kochendes Wasser gegeben 1 stunde dünsten gelassen.

Chocolate Cook (Notebook page 18)
4 egg yolks, 4 spoons of sugar, add 50g unpeeled almonds, 2 spoons of breadcrumbs, mixed in 2 teaspoons of softened chocolate, add foam from the whipped egg whites, some lemon juice. Grease the cake form with fat and crumbs and let it steam for 1 hour in boiling water.

Ingredients

    4 eggs
    60g granulated sugar
    60g almonds (unpeeled roasted and ground)
    30g breadcrumbs
    70g dark chocolate (melted)

Instructions

1. Beat the egg whites until stiff
2. Beat the egg yolks with sugar for about 5 minutes, add melted chocolate then add almonds and breadcrumbs and mix
3. Add the egg whites and mix lightly
4. Pour the mixture into a small, greased dish of 8" (22cm)
5. Place the dish in a larger baking form. Pour boiling water into the large form about 1" (2-3cm)
6. Steam in 350°F (180°C) oven for an hour

Chocolate Cook
JG

Chocolate Cook
JG

Chocolate Foam

Notebook page 47
IB

Chocolade Schaum Koch

8 dka Zucker wird mit 10 dka geriebenen Chocolade und 5 Eidotter flaumig gerührt, den Schnee von 3 Eiklar mit Mehl bestäubt leicht darunter gemengt und in ein Model welches früher gut ausgeschmiert und mit Biskuit ausgelegt gegeben und in Dunst gekocht.

Chocolate Foam (Notebook page 47)

80g sugar is mixed with 100g grated chocolate and 5 egg yolks until fluffy, the foam of 3 egg whites is lightly dusted with flour mixed in and placed in a form which is well greased and lined with biscuits. Bake in steam.

Chocolate Foam
JG

Ingredients

- 3 egg whites
- 5 egg yolks
- 80g granulated sugar
- 100g dark chocolate (grated)
- 20g flour (all purpose)
- 5-6 digestive biscuits

Instructions

1. Beat 3 egg whites until stiff
2. Beat 5 egg yolks with sugar until fluffy, add grated chocolate and keep beating for about 5 minutes
3. Fold in the egg whites lightly
4. Dust the mixture with the flour and mix
5. Pad the bottom of a well grease 8" (20cm) pie dish with crumbled biscuits
6. Pour the mixture on top of the biscuits
7. Place the dish in a larger baking pan. Pour boiling water into the large pan, about 1" (2-3cm)
8. Steam in 350°F (180°C) oven for 40 minutes

Chocolate Foam
JG

Rice Pudding

Notebook page 48
IB

Pudding von Reis

28 dka Reis wird 1 Liter Milch gekocht und ausgekühlt, 14 dka Butter wird mit 14 dka Zucker, 1 lemonie schale und 8 Eidotter flaumig abgetrieben, mit dem Reis gut vermengt und eine Weile gerührt 14 dka Zibeben und 14 dka fein gestiftelte Mandeln dazu gemengt und zuletzt den Schnee von 5 Ei klar leicht darunter vermengen, in ein ausgeschmiertes Model gegeben und ¾ Stunde in Dunst gekocht mit Weinchaudeau serviert.

Rice Pudding (Notebook page 48)

280g rice is boiled in 1 liter of milk and cooled, 140g butter is whipped with 140g sugar, 1 lemon peel and 8 egg yolks until fluffy, mixed well with the rice and stirred for a while, 140g raisins and 140g finely slivered almonds are added and finally mix in the foam from 5 egg whites, pour into a greased form and bake in steam for ¾ of an hour, serve with wine chaudeau.

Ingredients

- 140g white rice
- ½ liter milk
- 70g butter
- 70g granulated sugar
- 4 eggs
- zest from 1 lemon
- 70g raisins
- 70g slivered almonds (lightly roasted)

Rice Pudding
JG

Instructions

1. Cook the rice in the milk until soft and let it cool
2. Beat the softened butter with the sugar, the egg yolks and lemon zest until fluffy
3. Mix the butter with the cooked rice and stir
4. Add the slivered almonds and the raisins and stir well
5. Beat the egg whites into a stiff foam and mix lightly with the rice/butter mixture
6. Pour the mixture into a well greased baking form
7. Place the dish in a larger baking form. Pour boiling water into the large form about 1" (2-3cm)
8. Steam in moderate oven 350°F (180°) for 50 minutes
9. Let the pudding cool and turn it over onto a plate
10. Can be served with wine chaudeau

Moor in Shirt

Notebook page 47
IB

Mohr im Hemd

17 dka Zucker wird mit 6 Eidotter 21 dka geriebenen Mandeln und 7 dka Chocolade, Welche früher mit etwas Wasser aufgekocht, und ausgekühlt wird, dazu flaumig abgetrieben, den Schnee von 4 Eiklar leicht dazu verrührt und in einer ausgeschmierten Form in Dunst gekocht. Dann von 4 Eiklar den Schnee auf der Herde auf folgende Art gemacht: Man stellt den Schnee Kessel in ein kochendes Wasser und gibt die Eiklar 4 Eier schwer Zucker und 2 Löffel Rum hinein. Schlägt den Schnee fortwährend bis derselbe fest wird, nun begrenzt den koch damit und so wird derselbe zur Tafel gegeben.

Moor in shirt (Notebook page 47)

Whip until fluffy 170g sugar with 6 egg yolks, 210g ground almonds and 70g chocolate, which was previously boiled with a little water and cooled down, lightly stir in the foam of 4 egg whites and bake in a greased form in steam. Then from 4 egg whites make foam on the stove in the following way: Put the bowl in boiling water and add to the egg whites 4 eggs heavy sugar and 2 tablespoons of rum. Keep beating the foam until it hardens, now encircle the co it and so it is served to the table.

Ingredients

- 4 egg whites
- 6 egg yolks
- 120g granulated sugar
- 70g melted dark chocolate
- 210g almonds (lightly roasted finely ground)

Cream

- 4 egg whites
- 100g confectioners' sugar
- 2 tbs rum

Moor in Shirt
JG

Instructions

1. Beat the 4 egg whites to a stiff foam (keep 2 egg whites for the cream)
2. Whisk 6 egg yolks with sugar until fluffy, add melted chocolate and keep beating for 5 minutes
3. Add the finely ground almonds
4. Fold in the egg whites lightly
5. Pour the mixture into a well greased baking form
6. Place the form in a larger pan. Pour boiling water into the large pan about 1" (2-3cm)
7. Steam in 350°F (180°) oven for 55 minutes
8. Let the pudding cool and turn it over into a bowl

The Cream

1. Beat the egg whites with the sugar to a stiff foam, over a steam bowl
2. Add rum and keep beating until the foam hardens
3. Encircle the pudding with the cream and serve to the table

Mohr im Hemd is an Austrian confectionery. Chocolatier Jacques Torres claims to have invented the dish, but Jean-Georges Vongerichten disputes him vehemently, saying that he accidentally pulled a chocolate sponge cake out of the oven before it was finished and discovered a runny center. It is sold worldwide under the name Lava Cake [1].

Some argue that the term *Mohr* is discriminatory due to historical reasons. Defenders of the term counter by stating that Mohr is an outdated term used almost exclusively in art like in Othello and sayings like the famous quotation from Schiller (*Der Mohr hat seine Schuldigkeit getan, der Mohr kann gehen* – "The Moor has done his duty, the Moor can go."

Rassismus-Debatte um Mohr im Hemd in Österreich
www.krone.at, 21.06.2020

The racial connotations of the dish's name have drawn controversy. In 2012, the human rights organization **SOS Mitmensch** publicly criticized the name, suggesting replacements such as *Kuchen mit Schlag* or *Othello im Hemd*.

1. Budafoki Tamás, *(2022, March 23)*, A süti neve: mór ingben! Kóstolta már? *Matusz-Vad Zrt.*, https://blog.matusz-vad.hu/mohr-im-hemd-sutemeny-mor-ingben/

5

Cookies

Cookie-like hard wafers have existed for as long as baking is documented, in part because they survive travel very well. Early cookies were usually not sweet enough to be considered cookies by modern standards.

Sweet cookies seem to have their origins in 7th century Persia, shortly after the use of sugar became relatively common in the region. They spread to Europe through the Muslim conquest of Spain. By the 14th century, they were common in all levels of society throughout Europe, from royal cuisine to street vendors. The first documented instance of the figure-shaped gingerbread man was at the court of Elizabeth I of England in the 16th century. She had the gingerbread figures made and presented in the likeness of some of her important guests.

Christmas Cookies
JG

Cookies in Europe are tightly linked to Christmas. This can be traced to recipes from Medieval Europe biscuits, when many modern ingredients such as cinnamon, ginger, black pepper, almonds and dried fruit were introduced into the west. By the 16th century Christmas biscuits became popular across Europe, with *Lebkuchen* being favoured in Germany and *pepparkakor* in Sweden, while in Norway *krumkake* were popular.

It is a fun activity to bake cookies with my grandchildren. We are having a great time and get the rewards at the end when the cookies are ready, hot from the oven. It is also my chance to have quite time to communicate with my otherwise constantly active grandchildren.

Maya eating cookies The recipe from her great great grandmother
JG

Baking has huge benefits to kids. Hands on cooking activities help children develop confidence and skill. Following recipes encourages children to be self-directed and independent It also teaches them to follow directions and develop problem-solving skills. Baking also helps children's fine motor and eye-hand coordination skills by chopping, mixing, squeezing, and spreading.

So far, we have tried the following cookie recipes from my grandmother's notebook:

    Chocolate Kisses

    Linzer Cookies

    Date Kisses

    Vanilla Crescents

    Friends of the House

    Hussar Doughnuts

Chocolate Kisses

Notebook page 23
IB

Csokoládé Csók

12dkg cukor, 2 tojásfehérjével tűzön habosra verjük, 12dkg részelt csokoládé, 12dkg hosszúra vágott mandulát bele keverni, ostyán sütjük.

Chocolate Kisses (Notebook page 23)

120gram sugar, beaten overheat with 2 egg whites until fluffy, 120gram grated chocolate, 120gram long cut almonds mixed in, bake on a wafer oven.

Ingredients

2 egg whites
80g granulated sugar
120g grated chocolate
120g slivered or sliced almonds

Chocolate Kisses in the oven
JG

Instructions

1. Roast the almonds lightly
2. Beat egg whites to foam over steam heat, add sugar and continue beating for about 5 minutes
3. Add grated chocolate, almonds and mix
4. Place a teaspoon full of mixture on a parchment paper lined baking sheet
5. Bake in a low, preheated oven of 325°F (160°C) for 20-25 minutes, or longer if you like the kisses dryer

Linzer Cookies

Notebook page 11
IB

Linzer Aufgeriebenes

50deka Butter, 75deka Mehl, 38deka Zucker, 1/4kilo Mandeln, 10 gekochte Dotter, werden mit Allen aufgetrieben, ½ Zitronen Saft und schale, 4 rohe Dotter, um 5 x säuere Obers mit Allen zusammen geknetet, und dann ausgewalgt mit Formen ausgestrochen, obenauf in Ei weiß getauter Mandeln und Hagelzucker behandelt.

Linzer Cookies (Notebook page 11)

500g butter, 750g flour, 380gram sugar, 250g almonds, 10 boiled yolks, are shredded in a sieve, ½ lemon juice and peel, 4 raw yolks, about 5 x sour cream kneaded together, and then rolled out and stamp out with shapes. On top sprinkle with almonds thawed in egg whites and with pearl sugar.

Ingredients

250g butter (soft)
400g flour
125g granulated sugar
250g almonds (finely ground unpeeled)
1/2 lemon juice and zest
5 egg yolks (boiled)
2 egg yolks (raw)
Sour cream
1 cup raspberry jam

Linzer Cookies
JG

Instructions

1. Whisk the softened butter with the sugar
2. Mash the boiled egg yolks through a sieve into the butter
3. Add lemon zest and juice, and raw egg yolks and mix well
4. In a separate bowl mix the flour and the ground almonds
5. Pour the dry ingredients into the butter and knead together until smooth.
6. If too dry, add some sour cream until the dough is firm
7. Divide the dough into 2 equal parts (part for the bottoms and part for the tops) and refrigerate for 2 hours
8. Roll out the dough on a floured surface to cut out the cookie bottoms and tops
9. Preheat the oven to 350F° (180C°)
10. Bake the cut-outs on a parchment paper lined baking sheet for 15-20 minutes, or until the edges are pink
11. Spread raspberry jam on top of each cookie bottom and stack the top on each
12. Sprinkle with powder sugar

In 1653, the **Linzer Tart** recipe was discovered in the cookery manuscript of Countess Anna Margarita Sagramosa of Verona. It is known to be the earliest written cake recipe found.

The tart was baked like a pie with a delicious buttery almond crust, filled with black currant preserves and topped with a latticework crust. The recipe was developed using a crust made of nuts since they were easier to come by at times than wheat for flour.

Linzer Cookies
JG

In the Austrian city of Linz, bakers came up with a cookie version they could stock in their shops and it became a Christmas holiday tradition to see these lovely treats in the frosty windows.

The bakers would mix up a batch of Linzer torte dough, but instead of making a pie, they would cut out shapes such as stars, circles or hearts. Half of the shapes would get second cut-outs in the center. These dessert artisans constructed sandwich cookies using a whole cookie and a cut-out cookie. In the middle, they would place the black or red currant preserves just like the tart. After the cookie is put together, the jam or preserves peek through the Linzer eye to make a beautiful dessert, perfect for the holidays.

Date Kisses

Notebook page 23
IB

Datolya csók (Irén néni)
3 tojásfehérje, 25dkg cukor fél óráig keverni 25dkg mandula, 25dkg magjával mért datolya hosszura lesz vágva összekeverve és lassú tűznél sütve.

Date Kiss - Aunt Irén (Notebook page 23)
Mix 3 egg whites, 250g of sugar for half an hour, add 250g of almonds, mix in 250g dates, measured with seeds and cut lengthwise, and bake over low heat.

Date Kisses
JG

Ingredients
- 3 egg whites
- 60g granulated sugar
- 150g dates (measured with seeds)
- 150g almonds (slivered or sliced)

Instructions
1. Roast the almonds lightly
2. Cut dates in half, remove seeds, cut each half again
3. Beat the egg whites to foam, add sugar and continue beating for about 5 minutes
4. Add almonds and dates and mix
5. Place a teaspoon full of mixture on a parchment paper lined baking sheet
6. Bake in a low preheated oven 325°F (180°C) for 20-25 minutes

Vanilla Crescent

Notebook page 65
IB

Vanillen Kipferln
24dka Butter wird mit 14dka Zucker und 2 Dottern flaumig gerührt, dann mit 28dka Mehl und einer ¼ Stange Vanille nebst 10dka feingestoßenen Mandeln gut verarbeitet mit einem Messer auf dem Brette, wuzle dicke Nudeln daraus, forme sie zu kleinen Kipferln und backe sie schön gelb, dann bestreut man sie mit Vanille Zucker.

Vanilla Crescent (Notebook page 65)
240g butter is stirred with 140g sugar and 2 yolks until fluffy, then with 280g flour and a ¼ stick of vanilla along with 100g finely ground almonds, well processed. With a knife on the board, roll thick noodles out of it, form them into small croissants and bake them nice and yellow, then sprinkle with vanilla sugar.

> These crescent-shaped cookies originate from Vienna, Austria, where they are a much-loved, traditional Christmas cookies. They are also quite common throughout Europe, particularly in Germany, Hungary, Slovakia, and the Czech Republic. Legend has it that their shape was created to resemble the Turkish crescent moon, to celebrate one of the victories of the Hungarians and Austrians over the Turkish army.

Ingredients

- 240g butter (soft)
- 80g granulated sugar
- 2 egg yolks
- 280g flour (all purpose)
- 100g almonds (roasted, finely ground)
- 1/2 tbs vanilla extract
- Confectioners' / vanilla sugar

Instructions

1. Stir the butter with the sugar and the egg yolks until fluffy
2. Add the flour and mix completely
3. Add ½ tbs vanilla extract and the ground almonds
4. Work everything together completely into a soft dough
5. Refrigerate the dough for a couple of hours to keep the butter firm
6. Roll the dough to a long sausage and cut it up to small slices
7. Create from each slice a small noodle and shape it to a crescent
8. Bake in a preheated oven of 350°F (180°C) for 15 minutes or until the crescent tips became golden-brown
9. Let them cool and cover the crescent with confectioner / vanilla sugar

Vanilla Crescents
JG

Traditionally, *Vanillekipferl* are made with ground walnuts which result in a moister texture, but ground almonds or hazelnuts can also be used. Ground blanched almonds will result in a light-colored cookie whereas walnuts and hazelnuts will result in a darker, speckled cookie.

Vanilla Crescents
JG

Vanilla sugar adds a distinct flavor to these cookies. Vanilla sugar is just sugar that has been flavored with vanilla. It is common in many European baking recipes and can be found in little packets in the stores. However, if you cannot find it the store, it is easy to make yourself:

Vanilla sugar (Dr. Oetker)
JG

    4 cups confectioners' sugar
    1 vanilla bean (7-9 inches long)
    Place sugar (granulated or confectioners') in a 1-liter glass jar that has a tight-fitting screw-on lid
    Cut vanilla bean so it fits into jar and push it down into the sugar
    Place lid tightly on jar and allow to sit for at least 3 days before using

Friends of the House

Notebook page 13
IB

Hausfreunde

2 ganze Eier, 3 ½ Löffel Zucker, ¼ Zitronenschale, ¼ Stunde rühren, hernach 3 Löffel Mehl hinein, wieder gut durchrühren, dann 2 Handvoll gewaschene, getrocknete ganze Mandeln hinein. Nicht zu lange in einem ausgeschmierten Model backen. Tags darauf in dünnen Scheiben schneiden, von beiden Seiten gut mit Vanillezucker betreuen und in der Röhre auf einem Blech trocknen lassen.

Friends of the House (Notebook page 13)

2 whole eggs, 3½ spoons of sugar, ¼ lemon zest, stir for ¼ hour, then add 3 spoons of flour, stir well again, then add 2 handfuls of washed, dried whole almonds. Do not bake too long in a greased baking pan. The next day, cut into thin slices, cover with vanilla sugar on both sides and leave to dry in the oven on a baking sheet.

Ingredients

- 2 eggs
- 40g granulated sugar
- 1 lemon peel (roughly shaved)
- 100g almonds (whole, with skin, washed and dried)
- 40g flour
- Confectioner's sugar

Instructions

1. Beat the whole eggs with the sugar until thick and creamy
2. Add the lemon peel and keep beating
3. Mix in the almonds and the raisins
4. Add the flour and mix lightly
5. Spread the mixture on a well greased (or parchment lined) square 9" (23cm) baking pan - about 0.5" (1.5cm) height
6. Bake in a preheated 320°F (160°C) oven for 20-25 minutes
7. Let it cool for 10 minutes and cut into 1.5" (4cm) long rectangles, while still warm
8. Sprinkle with confectioner's sugar and let the biscuits dry in the oven on low heat 250°F (120°C) for 50 minutes, while turning them to from side to side
9. Store in an airtight container

Friends of the House
JG

PASTRIES FROM THE PAST ~ 81

Friends of the House
JG

Hausfreunde means "friends of the house". They are perfect biscotti for people who love dried fruit, hazelnuts and almonds and the best friends we could have at home to delight our palate. *Hausfreunde* is one of the traditional South Tyrolean Christmas cookies. Apparently, they don't look like much but don't be fooled, these are really something else entirely. They are crunchy on the outside and soft on the inside.

In Italy they are called *tozzette* - typical biscuits of Umbria and can be compared also to the famous **Sienese cantucci**. A genuine Tuscan meal always ends with a glass of *Vin Santo*, a wonderful Italian dessert wine, and a plate of *cantucci*. The cookies are dipped into the wine quickly so that they absorb its sweet aromas and a superficial coating of moisture but maintain crunchiness in the mouth[1].

These biscotti are very popular cookies during the Christmas holidays. Instead of almonds they can be prepared with hazelnuts and with or without chocolate or with the addition of other dried fruit such as raisins.

1. Dylan Garret, (2019, December 18), Tuscany's Cantucci, WhineEnthusiast, https://www.winemag.com/recipe/tuscanys-cantucci/

Hussar Doughnuts

Notebook page 72
IB

Husaren Krapfen

14dka Butter treibt man flaumig ab und gibt 2 Dotter, 7dka Zucker und 17 ½ dka Mehl dazu, dann werden kleine Kugeln gemacht, im jedes eine Vertiefung mit dem Finger gedrückt, mit Ei bestrichen und mit gehackten Mandeln bestreut, schön gelb gebacken, in jeder Marmelade.

Hussar Doughnuts (Notebook page 72)

140g butter is blended until fluffy then add 2 yolks, 70g sugar and 175gram flour, then make small balls, a depression is made in each of them with your finger. Coated with egg and sprinkled with chopped almonds, bake nice and yellow, fill in each marmalade.

Hssar Doughnuts in the oven
JG

Ingredients

140g butter (soft)
60g granulated sugar
2 egg yolks
175g flour (all purpose)
20g almonds (blanched and chopped)
30g jam (usually red)

Hussar Doughnuts
JG

Hussar Doughnuts
JG

Instructions

1. Stir the butter until fluffy
2. Add the egg yolk and keep stirring
3. Stir in the sugar and then slowly add the flour while mixing
4. Chill the dough for 1 hour
5. Dust your hand with flour and create small balls, of 1" (2.5cm) - about 20 - and place them on a parchment paper lined baking sheet
6. Make an indentation in each ball with your finger or the handle of a wooden spoon
7. Coat each cookie with egg and sprinkle with chopped almonds
8. Bake in a preheated oven of 350°F (180°C) for 35 - 40 minutes or until pink
9. Let them cool and fill the center of each cookie with jam

Hussars is the name for the members of the Hungarian cavalry from as early as the Magyar tribes to the cavalry of the Kingdom of Hungary. The Imperial and Royal Hussars made up the cavalry of the Austro-Hungarian Army from 1867 to 1918. The Hussars had high social prestige and colorful uniforms. My grandfather served in the Austro-Hungarian army during WWI as a cavalry officer.

Gandfather Fülöp, 1916, Bltojan Albania
JG

Maybe the cookies' name is related to the Hussars military uniform buttons. In Hungarian these cookies are also named "military button".

Hussar Doughnuts are also one of the traditional Christmas cookies in Austria. Writings from the second half of the 19th century describe the preparation for "*Husaren-Krapferln*", which has remained almost unchanged to this day: "Butter is quenched with yolk; sugar is added with vanilla… flour. When you have made small balls of it, you press a depression in each one, brush it with egg and sprinkle sugar and almonds on it, put the stewed fruit in the depression."

For the modern version, the doughnuts are filled with any heated, firm jam. Some recipes call for filling the jam before baking - others after baking. Finely grated (peeled and roasted) hazelnuts can also be worked into the short crust pastry.

6

Coffee Cakes

The sweet, crumbly companion to our morning coffee comes from the European coffeehouse tradition. The origins of the custom can be traced back to the 17th century when coffee was first imported to Germany. **Coffee Cakes** became popular in German, Dutch, and Scandinavian communities where they began to pair spiced sweet breads with the new drink.

Vienna Café Central
JG

By the 19th century, European coffeehouses commonly served sweet breads, small cakes, and cookies with their coffees – often to balance the bitterness of the coffee. Many of these coffeehouses were opening also in Vienna, Prague, and Budapest – making the term **Coffee Cake** much more widespread.

Café Gerbeaud, Budapest
JG

While some early versions of the dessert did contain coffee, the cake is meant to be an accompaniment to coffee. Most Coffee Cakes have simple cinnamon fillings, with some variations using chocolate, nuts, fruit or cream cheese. Both yeast and baking powder can be used to give lift to the cakes, with some versions presented as a braided ring or lattice-style.

In Germany there are regional variations, some of which include intricate cakes with layers of chocolate, whipping cream, cherries or jam. A ritual called *kaffeeklatsch* emerged, where people would gather for caffeine, sugar, and neighborhood gossip.

The hole in the middle of the coffee cake seems to be a more recent innovation, becoming popular in the 1950s with the Bundt pan. The idea behind the Bundt pan was to allow heavier batters and fillings to cook the whole way through while ensuring that the dough baked completely.

Bundt pan
JG

From my grandmother's notebook, I tried 6 cakes that fit the definition of Coffee Cake:

Bundt Cake, Simple
Anise Bread
Wreath
Brown Linzer Tort
Chocolate Bake
Nuts Cake with Chocolate Icing

Bundt Cake, Simple

Notebook page 35
IB

Gugelhupf, Einfach
Einfach aber gut! 14dka Butter wird mit 2 Eidotter flaumig abgetrieben, 3 Löffel Vanillezucker, 2dka Hefe, etwas salz, 2 drittel Liter Mehl, 1 drittel Liter lauwarm milch gut verrührt, zuletzt vermischt man 5dka Cibeben darunter und in ein mit Butter ausgeschmiert und gestiftelten Mandeln ausgelegtes Model bis zu Hälfte gefüllt so lange aufgehen bis das Modell voll ist und langsam ¾ stunden backen lassen, sofort ausgestürzt und mit Vanille Zucker bestreut.

Bundt Cake Simple (Notebook page 35)
Simple but good! Whisk 140g butter until fluffy with 2 egg yolks, 3 tablespoons of vanilla sugar, 20g yeast, a little salt, 350g of flour, 300 ml of lukewarm milk, stir well, finally you mix 50g raisins into. Fill in a butter smeared and sprinkled with slivered almonds baking form to half, let it rise until the form is full and bake slowly for 45 minutes, immediately turn it out and sprinkle it with vanilla sugar.

Ingredients

140g butter (soft)
2 egg yolks
350g flour
20g yeast - 10g active yeast
300ml milk (lukewarm)
3 tbs granulated sugar
50g raisins
½ tsp vanilla extract
Salt
Almonds (slivered)

Instructions

1. Whisk the butter with the egg yolks until fluffy
2. Add the flour, yeast, 3 tbs sugar, lukewarm milk and a little salt
3. Mix well and add the raisins
4. Grease a baking form with butter and sprinkle with slivered almonds
5. Fill the baking form halfway and let the dough rise until the form is full
6. Bake in a preheated oven of 325F° (170°C) for 45 minutes
7. When ready turn it out immediately and sprinkle with confectioner's sugar

Bundt Cake (Simple)
JG

Gugelhupf (Bundt Cake) is made from sponge cake or yeast dough, often marbled or with raisins. *Gugelhupf* is particularly popular in Austria and most of the successor states of the Austro-Hungarian Empire, Alsace, Southern Germany, Switzerland and Poland. Especially in Austria, *Gugelhupf* is not a name for a specific dough, but for the characteristic shape. It has a distinctive shape and is traditionally baked in a Bundt pan that has a circular hole in the middle.

"The Gugelhupf is still today an indispensable part of the Viennese family breakfast (especially on Sundays) and the Viennese coffee snack. The Gugelhupf, with or without raisins, marbled, with or without chocolate icing or in an old Viennese style with almonds, has long since become something like a bourgeois status symbol for prosperity". Franz Maier-Bruck, Kulinarisches Erbe Österreich

In late Medieval Austria, a *Gugelhupf* was served at major community events such as weddings, and was decorated with flowers, leaves, candles, and seasonal fruits. The name persisted through the Austro-Hungarian Empire, eventually becoming standardized in Viennese cookbooks as a refined, rich cake, flavored with rosewater and almond. The cake was popularized as a prestige pastry by Emperor Franz Joseph of Austria and by Marie-Antoinette in France.

Gugelhupf (Kugelhopf)
Amy Eber. Crawfish & Caramel

The earliest known *Gugelhupf* recipe is in a 1581 cookbook, *Ein neui Kochbuch*, by Marx Rumpolt, the cook who worked for several European courts in Bohemia and Hungary. He describes a "Hat Cake" with the distinctive shape and ornamentation, suggesting a similarity or imitation of the shape of a medieval hat.[1]

1. Thomas Stiegler, (2019, September 6), Cultural History of the Gugelhupf *Der Leiermann*, https://www.blog.der-leiermann.com/en/

Anise Bread

Anise Bread
JG

Anis Brot (Mama)

4 ganze eiere werden mit 20dk Zucker sehr gut abgetrieben. Dann 16dk Mehl und 1 Kaffee Löffel fein gestoßene Anis dazu.

Anise Bread - Mama (Notebook page 2)

4 whole eggs are stirred very well with 200g sugar. Then add 160g flour and 1 coffee spoon of finely crushed aniseed.

Ingredients

- 4 eggs
- 160g granulated sugar
- 160g flour (all purpose)
- 1 tsp ground aniseed

Instructions

1. Whisk the whole eggs and the sugar very well, until it is fluffy
2. Add the flour slowly and mix well
3. Add 1 tsp aniseed and mix
4. Grease a baking form with butter and fill it with the dough
5. Bake in a preheated oven of 350°F (180°C) for 45 minutes. When ready turn it out immediately and let it cool

Wreath

Notebook page 34
IB

Kranz

3Deka Hefe wird mit 4 Löffel lauer Milch, 2 Stück Würfelzucker und 1 Löffel Mehl aufgelassen, dann nimmt man 2/3 Liter Mehl, 1 gute Handvoll Zucker, die aufgegangene Hefe, etwas Salz und gieße dies in ein Drittel Liter laue Milch, mit einem ganzen Ei versprudelt und 10dka aufgelassene Butter dazu; dies alles mit dem Mehl gut ausarbeiten. Der Teig muss in der Feste eines Nockerl Teiges sein, schließlich gibt man 1 Handvoll Cibeben, welche darin gut verrührt sein müssen. 1 stunden aufgehen lassen, hernach dreht man von dem Teig einem armdicken Kranz auf ein Blech, eine Weile gehen lassen, dann mit Ei bestreichen, mit Mandeln, welche gestoßen sein müssen, bestreuen. Langsam backen und kalt zum Kaffee servieren.

Wreath (Notebook page 34)

30g yeast is added to 4 spoons of lukewarm milk, 2 pieces of sugar cubes and 1 spoonful of flour. Then take 350g flour, 1 good handful of sugar, the risen yeast, a little salt and pour this into a 330ml lukewarm milk 1 whole beaten egg and 100g melted butter with it; work all this out well with the flour. The dough must be in the solid like a dumpling dough, after all this you add a handful raisins, which must be well mixed in. Let it rise for 1 hour, then roll the dough into a wreath as thick as an arm on a baking tray, let it rise for a while, then brush with egg, sprinkle with almonds, which must be sliced, bake slowly, and serve cold with coffee.

Ingredients

30g yeast - 10g active yeast
350g flour (all purpose)
50g granulated sugar
100g butter (melted)
1 egg
330ml lukewarm milk
60g raisins
Salt
Almonds (slivered)

Wreath
JG

Instruction

1. Mix the yeast with 4 tbs milk, 1 tsp sugar and 1 tsp flour
2. Mix the flour, yeast, sugar with a little salt
3. Pour this mixture into the the lukewarm milk and add the melted butter and the whole egg
4. Knead into a dough, firm like a dumpling dough
5. Add the raisins and mix well
6. Let it rise for 1 hour
7. Form the dough into a roll as thick as your arm and lay it on buttered a baking tray in a circle and let it rise for a while
8. Brush with an egg and sprinkle with slivered almonds
9. Bake in a preheated oven of 325°F (170°C) for 45 minutes. Let it cool and serve with coffee

Brown Linzer Tart

Notebook page 59
IB

Bräune Linzer Torte

28 Deka Butter wird flaumig gerührt und mit 28 Deka Mehl gut abgebröselt, 28 Deka ungeschälte Mandeln feingestoßen, 28 Deka Zucker, 1 Lemoine die feingehackte schale und 1 Deka Zimt mit einigen Gewürznelken dazu vermischt, mit 3 Dotter und wenig Obers zu einem festen teig gemacht, mit Hilfe eines Messers ausgearbeitet. – Dies in 4 Teile geteilt, von 3 teilen 3 Blätter gemacht und von vierten Teil Gitter auf das obere Blatt, vorher jedoch mit Marmelade schmieren, dann langsam backen alle Blätter mit Salse schmieren und aufeinandersetzen, das Gitter kommt oben.

Brown Linzer Torte (Notebook page 59)

280g butter is stirred until fluffy and crumbled well with 280g flour, 280g unpeeled almonds finely crushed, 280g sugar, the finely chopped peel of 1 lemon, and 10gram cinnamon mixed with a few cloves, made into a firm dough with 3 yolks and a little sour cream, worked out with the help of a knife. - Divide this into 4 parts, make 3 sheets and the fourth part for the grid of the top sheet. But first smear the sheets with jam and put them on top of each other, slowly bake all the sheets, the grid comes on top.

Ingredients

- 250g butter (soft)
- 250g flour (all purpose)
- 125g granulated sugar
- 250g ground unpeeled almonds
- 1 lemon zest
- 10g cinnamon + ground cloves
- 2 egg yolks
- Sour cream
- 1 cup raspberry jam

Linzer Tart
JG

Instructions

1. Crumble the butter with the flour
2. Add the ground almonds, sugar, lemon peel, cinnamon and cloves
3. Make this into a firm dough with the egg yolks and sour cream
4. Divide the dough into 4 equal parts and roll out into 4 round sheets of 9" (22cm)
5. Spread raspberry jam on top of 3 sheets. Stack them on top of each other. From the last sheet create the grid
6. Line a baking pan with parchment paper and bake in a preheated oven of 350°F (180°C) for 20-25 minutes

---

In 1653, the **LinzerTart** recipe was discovered in the cookery manuscript of Countess Anna Margarita Sagramosa of Verona. The tart was baked like a pie with a delicious buttery almond crust, filled with black currant preserves and topped with a latticework crust.

There is a cookie version for this tart, invented in the city of Linz, which became a Christmas holiday tradition in Austria and Europe.

Chocolate Bake

Notebook page 4
IB

Chocolade Kuchen

¼ Pfund Butter, ¼ Pfund Zucker wird mit 4 Eier Dotter gut abgetrieben, ¼ Pfund Mandeln gebrüht und firm gestoßen, 4 Taferl Chocolade, ¼ Pfund Mehl und von klaren den Schnee kommt auch vermengt das Blech dünn mit Butter beschmiert hineingegeben und bei langsam Feuer gebacken. In Schnitte geschnitten mit Marmelade gefüllt, eines auf andere gegeben.

Chocolate Bake (Notebook page 4)

125g butter, 125g sugar, 4 eggs yolks well whipped, 125g almonds scalded and firmly pounded, 4 bars chocolate, 125g flour and from the egg whites firm foam is mixed in. In thinly buttered baking sheet, it is baked over slow fire. Cut into slices filled with jam, one on top of the other.

Ingredients

- 125g butter (soft)
- 100g + 25g granulated sugar
- 5 eggs
- 60g almonds (blanched, roasted and ground)
- 140g dark chocolate
- 125g flour (all purpose)
- ½ tsp baking powder

Dr. Oetker's baking powder - Backin
JG

Instructions

1. Beat butter with 100g sugar and egg yolks well, until light. Add melted chocolate and mix
2. Beat the egg whites with the remaining sugar
3. Add flour, baking powder and almonds to the chocolate mixture and mix lightly then fold in the the egg whites
4. Bake in a greased 10" (26cm) baking pan in a preheated oven 350°F (180°C) for 40 minutes

Chocolate Bake
JG

Although the original recipe does not include baking powder it is added here to make the dough light and airy. In the recipe book baking powder is mentioned for the first time on page 75, but I am sure it was already well used. Dr. Oetker Baking Powder has been a guarantee of successful baking for more than 100 years. In 1893 August Oetker came up with the ideal baking powder mixture which he called "Backin". The ingredients in the baking powder ensure that the dough is loose and light. One sachet was enough for 500g of flour.

Nuts Cake with Chocolate Icing

Notebook page 6
IB

Chocolade Torte
5 Eier werden mit ein ¼ Pfund Zucker flaumig abgetrieben, 6 Loth Mandeln, 6 Loth Nüsse kommen dazu verrührt, vom klaren den Schnee 1 Löffel Semmelbrösel, in dir Tortenform gebacken gegeben. Wenn's gebacken ist, Chocolade Glasur, die folgendermaßen gemacht wird: Guter schwarzer Kaffee, süß kochen gelassen und ein oder zwei Taferl Chocolade dazu, wenn es gut eingekocht ist, warm darüber gegeben.

Chocolate Cake (Notebook page 6)
5 eggs yolks are whisked with a 250gram sugar until fluffy, 90gram almonds, 90gram of nuts, beaten egg whites and 1 tablespoon of breadcrumbs, baked in the cake form. When it's baked, chocolate icing, which is made as follows: good black coffee, let it cook until sweet, then add a bar or two of chocolate. When it has boiled in, pour it warm over the cake.

Ingredients

- 5 eggs
- 150g granulated sugar
- 90g almonds (unpeeled roasted and ground)
- 90g walnuts (ground)
- 2 tbs breadcrumbs

Icing

- 1 shot espresso coffee (very short)
- 70g dark chocolate

Nuts Cake
JG

Instructions

1. Beat the egg whites to a stiff foam
2. Beat egg yolks with sugar about 5 minutes
3. Add breadcrumbs and nuts and mix well. Fold in the egg whites
4. Pour into a round greased Bunt baking form
5. Bake in preheated moderate oven 350°F (180°C) for 45 minutes
6. Let it cool

The Icing

1. Break small pieces of chocolate into hot coffee and mix until melted
2. Pour over cake

Nuts cake - walnuts and almonds
JG

7

Fruit Cakes

This section includes cakes from the recipe notebook with fruits as their dominant ingredient. The recipe book has a lot of complicated cakes based on nuts or flour and have various creams and icing. The cakes based on fruits are quite simple but dependent on the availability of the season's fruit.

The European continental climate in Slovakia and Hungary is very favorable for growing apples, cherries, plums, pears, peaches and apricots. Many of these fruits were used to make jams or brandy. Extensive vineyards in the Nitra region, produced huge amount grapes to make wine before WWII,

As my grandmother's notebook was maintained through the years, while she moved from Tapolcsány (Topoľčany) to Nitra, from Nitra to Bratislava, Zilina and to Budapest, obviously, the availability of produce depended on the local harvest and crop, her family's situation and the general political and economic conditions.

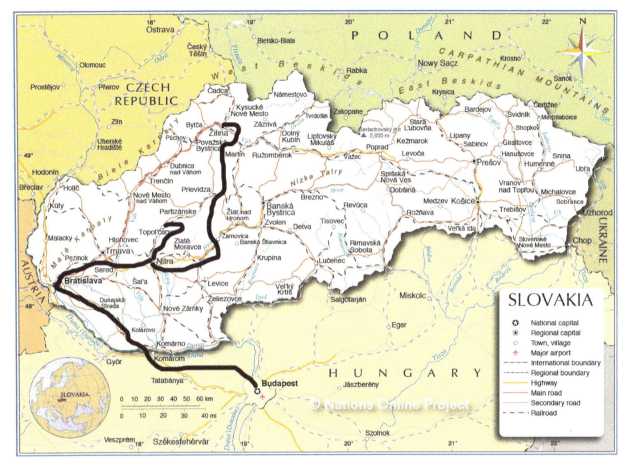

From Topoľčany to Budapest
JG

I picked 5 *Fruit Cake* recipes to include in this book:

Plum or Cherry Cake

Orange Cake

Apple Pie

Bishop's Bread

Plum or Cherry Cake

Notebook page 72
IB

Schlitz oder Kirschen Kuchen

4 Ei schwer Zucker, 4 Ei schwer Butter, 4 Ei schwer Mehl rührt erst die Butter mit dem Zucker flaumig ab, dann gibt man 1 Dotter nach dem andern dazu, dann langsam das Mehl und zuletzt den Schnee. Wenn die Masse schon in der Form ist, werden die Kirschen leicht eingeworfen.

Plum or Cherry cake (Notebook page 72)

4 eggs heavy sugar, 4 eggs heavy butter, 4 eggs heavy flour. First stir the butter with the sugar until fluffy, then add 1 yolk after the other, then slowly add the flour and finally the beaten egg whites. When the mixture is ready in the cake form, throw in the cherries lightly.

Cherries
JG

Ingredients

    150g granulated sugar
    4 eggs
    250g butter (soft)
    200g flour (all purpose)
    450g plums or cherries

Instructions

1. Pit the plums and quarter / pit the cherries
2. Beat the egg whites into a stiff foam
3. Stir the softened butter until fluffy
4. Add sugar and, then add egg yolks 1 at a time and keep beating until creamy
5. Slowly add the flour and finally fold in the beaten egg whites
6. Pour the mixture into greased 10" (26 cm) pan and spread the plums or cherries to sink into the batter
7. Bake in a preheated 350°F (180°C) oven for 45 minutes, lower temperature to 325°F (160°C) and keep baking another 15 minutes until fully baked

Cherry Cake
JG

Cherry Cake
JG

Plum Cake
JG

Schlitz – Damson Plum is a European plum - small round clingstone fruit with a deep blue/purple skin and spicy yellow flesh.

They are sweet enough to eat but also have some acidity which makes them less palatable than other varieties. They are excellent for cooking, preserving, making jam and a liqueur known as Slivovitz.

The name "damson" stems from the Latin *"damascenum"* meaning "plum of Damascus", make some people believe that this plum may have come from the ancient city of Damascus and was brought to England by the Romans. This theory has been highly contested because there is ample evidence that Damson plums have been grown in England much earlier.

Damson Plums
JG

Orange Cake

Notebook page 8
JG

Orangen Torte
6 Dotter, 4 Löffel Zucker, die leicht abgetriebene schale ein orange und den ganzen Saft eine ¼ Stunden rühren, nachher 2 Handvoll gebrühte gestoßene Mandeln, 3 Löffel Semmelbrösel hinein gut verrühren und dann den festen Schnee von 6 Eiweiß, bei mäßigem Feuer backen.

Orange Cake (Notebook page 8)
6 egg yolks, 4 spoons sugar, the lightly shaved orange peel with the all the juice to stir for ¼ hour. Then add 2 handful of roasted pounded almonds, 3 spoons of breadcrumbs, stir well and add the stiffly beaten foam of 6 eggs whites, bake in moderate heat.

Ingredients
6 eggs
100g +20g granulated sugar
150g almonds (ground)
3 tablespoons breadcrumbs or matza meal
½ cup orange juice (1 or 2 oranges)
Zest from 1 lemon & 1 orange

Topping
150g dark chocolate
15g butter
1-2 tablespoons boiling water

Orange Cake
JG

Instructions

1. Mix the breadcrumbs and juice. If the mixture is lumpy add more juice. Set aside
2. Beat the egg yolks with 100g sugar and zest for about 5 minutes
3. Beat the egg whites with the remaining sugar util stiff. Beat until the sugar dissolves. About 5 minutes
4. Mix two egg mixtures lightly, add the readcrumbs and finally the almonds
5. Pour into a well greased 10" (26 cm) baking pan
6. Bake in a preheated oven of 350°F (190°C) for 35 minute. Let it cool
7. Melt chocolate in the microwave. Add butter and stir until it melts Add 2-3 tablespoons of boiling water and mix well. Spread on the cake.

Orange Cake with Icing
JG

Apple Pie

Notebook page 9
IB

Apfel Torte
25 Deka Sueres oder 25 Deka March gut durcharbeiten, ½ Liter Mehl, ein ganzes Ei, ein bisschen Salz, Einen Esslöffel Zucker mit Wein zusammenkneten, ein Mürben Teig gemacht, etwas dicker als Messerrückendick auswalgen, 2 Theile geschnitten, einer größer als der andere, gefüllt mit Apfel, die in Wein, Zucker, Zitronenschale gedünstet werden. Wenn selbe ausgekühlt sind, 2 Handvoll gestoßene Nüsse, 2 Handvoll Cibeben.

Apple Pie (Notebook page 9)
250g Sueres or 250g March, work well, ½ liter flour, a whole egg, a bit of salt, knead a tablespoon of sugar with wine, make a short crust pastry, roll out a little thicker than the back of a knife, cut into 2 parts, one larger than the other, stuffed with apples stewed in wine, sugar, lemon zest. When they have cooled down add 2 handfuls of crushed nuts and 2 handfuls of raisins.

Ingredients

Filling
5 Apples (cored, peeled and sliced)
1 lemon juice and zest
1 tbs granulated sugar
25g walnuts (roughly crushed)
25g raisins
2 tbs red or white wine

Short Crust
250g flour (all purpose)
125g butter (soft)
1 egg
1 tbs sugar
Salt
2 tbs white wine

Instructions

The Filling

1. Peel and cut the apples
2. Add the lemon juice and zest
3. Add 1 tbs sugar
4. Simmer in a saucepan with the wine for 10 minutes, until the liquids have evaporated
5. Let it cool and add walnuts and raisins and mix well

Apple Pie
JG

The crust

1. Stir the butter until creamy
2. Add the flour and mix completely
3. Add sugar, salt and keep mixing
4. Knead together with 3 tbs white wine
5. Keep refrigerated for at least 2 hours, in two, not equal pieces
6. Roll out the larger part to the size of the pie dish
7. Fill with the cooked apples
8. Roll out the smaller part to cover the pie. Seal the edges at the pie dish
9. Bake in a preheated oven of 350°F (180°C) for 40 minutes

Apple Pie slice
JG

Bishop's Bread

Bischofs Brod 1

½ Pfund Mandeln, ½ Pfund Zucker, ¼ Pfund Rosinen, 1/8 Pfund Orangenschale, 4 Eier, die Eier mit dem Zucker 1 Stunde rühren, dann erst die Zutaten, nur noch dazu 18dkg Mehl. Das Blech entweder mit wachs oder mit Öl beschmieren.

Notebook page 24
IB

Bishop's Bread 1 (Notebook Page 24)

250g almonds, 250g sugar, 125g raisins, 70g orange peel, 4 eggs. Beat the eggs with the sugar for 1 hour, then add the ingredients, just then add 180g flour. Smear the baking pan with either wax or oil.

Bischofs Brod 2

18deka Mehl, 32deka Zucker, 4 ganze Eier und von speren den Schnee, in summa 8 Eier, 12 ½dkg Rosinen, 12 ½ Orangenschalen, Chocolade, 25dkg Mandeln, Haselnüsse, kurz alles was gut ist hineingeben.

Bishop's bread 2 (Notebook page 4)

180gram flour, 320gram sugar, 4 whole eggs and from saved egg whites add stiffly beaten foam, a total of 8 eggs, 125gram raisins, 125gram orange peel, chocolate, 250gram almonds, hazelnuts, in short everything that is good.

Notebook page 4
IB

My grandmother's recipe book has two very similar recipes for Bishop's Bread, the main difference is the extra spare egg whites you can add to the batter.

Ingredients

- 250g almonds blanched and slightly roasted
- 150g granulated sugar*
- 120g dried cherries
- 70g orange peel
- 50g dried cranberries or raisins
- 125g dark chocolate chips
- 4 eggs + any leftover egg whites
- 180g flour (all purpose)
- 1 tsp vanilla

*Adjust the amount of sugar to the other sweet ingredients - the dried fruits and chocolate chips

Bishop's Bread
JG

Instructions

1. Beat the eggs with sugar and vanilla well, then add the dried fruit and chocolate chips
2. Beat any leftover egg whites into foam and fold into the mixture
3. Mix in the flour quickly
4. Bake in a well-greased 6"x 12" (15 x 30 cm) loaf pan in 325F° (170C°) oven for 65 minutes

Bishop's Bread
JG

This **Bishop's Bread** is densely packed with all sorts of delicious ingredients, like blanched almonds, walnuts, raisins, cranberries chopped dates, chocolate chips, dried cherries, candied orange peel and/or any other dried fruit you have. There is just barely enough batter to hold everything together. If you have leftover whites from other baking/cooking, they can be whipped and folded into the mixture to help it rise. It is baked in a well-greased Bishop's Bread pan - a kind of loaf pan.

Bishop's Bread does not look or taste like a fruitcake. Some recipes also call it "Broken Glass", "Stained Glass" or "Jewel Bread" because all the dried cherries and chunks of chocolate are revealed when you cut it into a very thin slice, making it look like stained glass.

The history of Bishop's Bread isn't really clear, most likely originated from Croatia. There are many variations on the recipe, from around Northern Europe. Recipes for Bishop's Bread can be found in German cookbooks of the early 19th century; they describe the production of biscuit dough with raisins (*zibeben*) pinched (blanched) almonds and zest from citrus peel. In the middle of the century, recipe modifications became popular with such ingredients as chocolate chips, pine nuts, pistachios, and more. Sometimes, it is either sugar-coated or coated with apricot jam and covered with chocolate icing.

Bishop's Bread - stained glass
JG

8

Strudels

Strudel is a stuffed pastry from Austria, very popular in all former Austro-Hungarian countries (Austria, Hungary, Czech Republic) and in Germany and Alsace (France). It is the most iconic Austrian and Hungarian dessert, so it deserves a special chapter.

The strudel dough is special because the dough is very thinly wrapped around a heavy filling. Therefore, the challenge of a good authentic strudel dough is that it needs to be very thin and at the same time to be able to hold the heavy filling without breaking apart. It is a widely held belief that making strudel dough from scratch is difficult and time-consuming. It's not!

Many have been using puff pastry or Philo dough to prepare strudels because they can be easily bought ready made in the store. I've been told that this is completely wrong. It's prepared the same way as a noodle dough just that it calls for a lot of oil ---- the dough is left resting covered in oil for 1 hour. The oil and the egg make the dough super elastic so that you can roll and pull it out to a very thin layer.

The following table describes the differences:

Puff Pastry	Strudel Dough	Phyllo Dough
Butter is folded in	The oil is part of the dough from the beginning	Brushed with oil before being baked
Of French origin, probably inspired by the Arabic Phyllo dough	Consists of flour, water, egg and a lot of oil	Greek, Balkan and Middle Eastern crunchy thin dough
Butter layers are folded into the dough, and while baking the butter and steam create layers	Prepared the same way as a noodle dough just that it calls for a lot of oil and left standing covered in oil	Prepared with water and flour, rolled out and brushed with oil or butter before being layered and baked
Blows up and flaky soft, and fragile to the touch	The oil and the egg make the dough super elastic so that you can roll and pull it out to a very thin layer, so it can take that much filling without breaking	The tissue-thin layers make for flaky results but can also be challenging to work with

The Strudel is only a strudel with a strong crunchy thin layer wrapped around rich sweet fillings, like apples, nuts, cherries and poppy seeds or savory fillings like cheeses and cabbage. Only the strudel dough can take that much filling without breaking.

I tried a few of the strudel recipes in my grandmother's notebook and learned a lot about making the strudel dough, how to stretch it, how to fill and roll it up. I found that the following dough recipe is the most practical:

Ingredients (for two Strudel rolls)

280g flour (all purpose)
160ml water (lukewarm)
2 egg yolks
3 tbs vegetable oil
1 tsp vinegar
Salt
Flour for dusting

Instructions

1. Add half of the flour to a mixing bowl add and salt and mix well
2. Make a well in the center and add the lukewarm water
3. Add 2 tbs oil, egg yolks and vinegar
4. Mix the ingredients well until smooth
5. Add the rest of the flour and keep mixing to a smooth dough
6. Keep kneading well and long enough until the dough is not sticky
7. Keep kneading more on a floured surface for 10 minutes
8. The dough should be soft enough but firm. If too soft add more flour and if too stiff add a little water
9. Make 2 smooth balls of equal size. Cover them with the remaining oil all around
10. Let them rest for 1 hour in a warm place

Before filling the strudel rolls (repeat for the second dough ball)

1. Roll out the dough ball on a floured surface
2. When thin enough start to stretch the dough in the air with the back of your hands
3. Lay it on floured tea towel and keep stretching to a rectangle

Stretching the dough
Anat

Preparation Notes

1. The more you knead the strudel dough, the better as the gluten gets activated with the water, the force, and warmth. That will help the dough to stretch well
2. To test if your dough is ready, take it up into your hand and if it drops quickly, it's good
3. You can keep the dough refrigerated for 2 days
4. Stretch the dough on a floured tea towel or smooth tablecloth
5. Use the back of your hands, your knuckles, to stretch it while turning it round (remove all jewelry first) – like pizza dough
6. Let the dough rest a minute between stretches
7. When all drawn out to a rectangle remove the ticker edges to keep the thin dough even

In my grandmother's notebook the are several strudel recipes. I included in this section:

Apple Strudel
Almond Strudel
Poppy Seed Strudel

Almond Strudel
JG

Apple Strudel

Notebook page 39
IB

Apfel Pittah
28dka Butter wird mit Hilfe eines Messers in 56dka Mehl verarbeitet, dann 1 Löffel Zucker mit 3 Eidotter dazwischen gemengt und etwas salz dazu geben, mit dem Nudelwalker gut ausgearbeitet, die Hälfte des Teiges auf ein Blech ausgewalkt und mit folgende Maße bestriechen: 15 Äpfel werden geschält und in Scheiben geschnitten, 25dka Zucker mit etwas Wasser befeuchtet und dick eingekocht, dann die Äpfel hinein gegeben und unter beständigem rühren solange kochen lassen bis dies einer Dicke von Kindskoch wird, dann last es kalt werden (beim Kochen gibt man Lemonie Schalen hinein) dann werden 8dka Cibeben dazu gemengt, und nun wird das Püree auf dem Teig gestrichen, due andere Hälfte des Teiges darauf gelegt, oben Gitter von Teig gemacht, mit grob gestoßenen Mandeln bestreut un gebacken. Mit Zucker oben bestreuen und zerschneiden.

Apple Pittah (Notebook page 39)
280g butter is processed with a knife in 560g flour, then 1 spoonful of sugar mixed with 3 egg yolks in between and add some salt, work out well with the pasta roller, roll out half of the dough on a baking sheet and spread with the following mixture: 15 apples peeled and sliced, 250g sugar moistened with a little water and boiled down thickly, then add the apples and cook, stirring constantly, until it becomes a child's boil thickness, then let it cool (when cooking, add lemon zest) then 80g raisins are mixed in, and now the puree is spread on the dough, the other half of the dough is placed on top, lattices of dough are made on top, sprinkled with coarsely crushed almonds and baked. Sprinkle with sugar on top and cut up.

Prepare strudel dough for two rolls – recipe on page 115

Ingredients for 2 Strudel Roll fillings
- 10 apples (about 2kg), (peeled and sliced)
- 100g granulated sugar
- 80g raisins
- 1 lemon zest
- 140g butter (melted)

Instructions
The Filling

Apple Strudel
JG

Ambrosia apples cooked

1. Cook the sugar with a little water until it becomes thick
2. Add the peeled and sliced apples and stir frequently until the apples are soft and most liquids evaporated
3. Mix in the zest of a lemon and the raisins
4. Let it cool

The Strudel

1. Sprinkle the thinly drawn strudel dough with melted butter
2. Spread the filling evenly onto half of the dough, 1.5" (3 cm) from the edges
3. Sprinkle melted butter over the filling and fold in 3 sides of the rectangle
4. Roll up the strudel with the help of the tea towel and brush with melted butter on each turn and put the strudel roll on a parchment paper lined baking tray, with the seam down
5. Brush with the remaining melted butter and bake in a preheated oven of 375°F (190°C) oven or 25-30 minutes

Apple Strudel is an oblong pastry with apple filling inside. The filling is made of sliced apples, sugar, cinnamon, raisins, and breadcrumbs. A juicy *Apfelstrudel* should be baked with good ripe apples that are tart, crisp, and aromatic.

The strudel gained popularity in the 18th century through the Habsburg Empire (1278-1780) but probably related to the Turkish baklava pastry, introduced into Austria in 1453. Gradually strudels with different fillings were created. The *Apfelstrudel* was the favorite dessert of Empress Sisi and Crown Prince Rudolf and it is considered to be the national dish of Austria. Strudel is also a traditional pastry in the areas previously owned by the Austro-Hungarian Empire.

The oldest Strudel recipe is from 1696, a handwritten recipe for a milk-cream strudel, now preserved at The Vienna City and State Library (*Wiener Stadtbibliothek*).

Apple Strudel
JG

According to the *Schönbrunn's Apfelstrudel* show (a show at the café in the Habsburg's royal palace in the outskirts of Vienna) that demonstrates how to make the "royal and official" version of the *ApfelstrudelI*, the secret is using sunflower seed oil. This makes the dough highly flexible and elastic.

Apple Strudel Show at Schönbrunn Palace, Vienna
JG

The name Strudel comes from the German word for "whirlpool" or "eddy". The rolled version of the pastry looks like the inside of a whirlpool.

Almond Strudel

Notebook page 38
IB

Mandel Strudel

28dka Mehl, ein eigroßes Stück Butter, 2 Eidotter, 2 Würfel Zucker, in etwas lauwarme Wasser und etwas Salz auflassen dies zum einen strudelteig kneten, gut ausarbeiten, dann unter ein gewärmtes rein ½ Stunden rasten lassen. 21dka Butter mit 8 Eidotter flaumig abtrieben, 14dka fein gestoßene Mandeln, von einer Lemoine die Schale, 21dka Zucker, und von 6 Ei klaren Schnee leicht dazu vermengt, in den dünn angezogen Strudel gleichmäßig füllen, zusammenrollen und im einen mit Brösel und Butter ausgeschmierten rein gebacken, oben mit Butter öfters geschmiert und mit Vanille Creme servieren.

Almond Strudel (Notebook page 38)

280g flour, an egg-sized piece of butter, 2 egg yolks, 2 sugar cubes melted in little lukewarm water with a little salt. 210g butter stirred with 8 egg yolks until fluffy, 140g finely ground almonds, the zest of a Lemoine, 210g sugar, and foam from 6 egg whites lightly mixed, fill evenly into the thinly drawn strudel dough, roll it up and put in a greased with butter and spread with breadcrumbs to bake smeared with butter on top. Serve with vanilla cream.

Prepare strudel dough for two rolls – recipe on page 115

Ingredients for 2 Strudel Roll fillings
- 200g butter (soft)
- 6 eggs
- 140g almonds (roasted, finely ground)
- 100g sugar
- 1 lemon zest
- 140g butter (melted)

Almond Strudel
JG

Instructions
The Filling

1. Stir the butter with the sugar and egg yolks until creamy
2. Add the finely ground almonds
3. Mix in the zest of a lemon
4. Whip the egg whites until it is a stiff foam
5. Fold lightly the egg whites into the butter almond mixture

The Strudel

1. Brush the thinly drawn, rectangle, strudel dough with melted butter
2. Spread the filling evenly onto half of the dough, 1.5" (3 cm) from the edges
3. Sprinkle melted butter over the filling
4. Fold in 3 sides of the rectangle
5. Roll up the strudel with the help of the tea towel and brush with melted butter on each turn and put the strudel roll on a parchment paper lined baking tray, with the seam down
6. Brush with the remaining melted butter and bake in a preheated oven of 375°F (190°C) oven or 25-30 minutes

Poppy Seed Strudel

Notebook page 38
IB

Mohnstrudel
Es wird ein gewöhnliche strudelteig verfertigt, dünn ausgezogen, 6 Eidotter in etwas mehr als ein Drittel Milchrahm ab gesprudelt, 2 drittel Liter Mohn fein gestoßen und mit 14dka Zucker vermengt, 10dka Mandeln, welche gerieben sein müssen und 10dka cibeben darunter gemischt, 28dka Butter wird auf gelassen, der Teig damit gut bespritzt, dann streut man den Mohn darauf, Welcher mit dem dickt gekocht Zucker und dem Rahm vermischt sein muss, überall gleichförmig darauf schmieren, mit Butter abermals rechts bespritzen, zusammenrollen und backen.

Poppy Seed Strudel (Notebook page 38)
An ordinary strudel dough is made, stretched out thinly, 6 egg yolks boiled in a little more than 1/3 liter whipping cream, 2/3 liter of poppy seeds finely crushed and mixed with 140g sugar, 100g almonds, which must be grated and 100g raisins mixed in, 280g butter melted, to sprinkle the dough with it, then one spreads the poppy seeds on it, which must be mixed with the thickly boiled sugar and the cream, smear evenly all over it, sprinkle with butter again, roll up and bake.

Prepare strudel dough for two rolls – recipe on page 115

Ingredients for 2 Strudel Roll fillings
    350ml whipping cream
    6 egg yolks
    200g poppy seeds (finely ground)
    100g almonds (finely ground
    100g granulated sugar
    100g raisins
    140g butter (melted)

Poppyseed Strudel
JG

Instructions
The Filling

1. Boil the whipping cream with 6 egg yolks
2. Mix the poppy seeds with sugar and add to the whipping cream
3. Add the finely ground almonds
4. Keep cooking until it gets thick, stirring all the time
5. Remove from heat and keep stirring
6. Mix in the raisins and let the filling cool

Poppyseed filling
JG

The Strudel

Strudel ready to bake
JG

1. Brush the thinly drawn strudel dough with melted butter
2. Spread the filling evenly onto half of the dough, 1.5" (3 cm) from the edges
3. Sprinkle melted butter over the filling and fold in 3 sides of the rectangle
4. Roll up the strudel with the help of the tea towel and brush with melted butter on each turn and put the strudel roll on a parchment paper lined baking tray, with the seam down
5. Brush with the remaining melted butter and bake in a preheated oven of 375°F (190°C) oven for 25-30 minutes

Poppyseed Strudel
JG

9

Salty Pastries

After all the sweet cakes, cookies and tarts, I am sure you also want a little salty taste. The recipe notebook has quite a few salty sticks, croissants, scones and bows – some really simple and others more sophisticated.

Here I have 3 recipes for formal events and casual get together with family and friends. Or just to have a bite or a snack:

Crumbly Croissant

Pretzel Sticks

Butter Scones

Many salty pastry recipes use quark - cheese curds or butter to make them interesting. Cheese curds (*topfen*) are easily available in Europe but not in North America. So, the salty pastries in this section are made with a lot of butter.

The job of butter in baking (besides being delicious) is to give richness, tenderness and structure to cookies, cakes, pies and pastries. We alter the way butter works in a recipe by changing its temperature and choosing when to combine it with the other ingredients. For example, the same butter makes things fluffy when creamed with sugar but creates airy pockets between layers of thin dough for perfectly flaky pie crust when ice-cold cubes are cut into dry flour.

Salt and spices like caraway and cumin seeds are intended to give the pastry its distinct taste.

Salty Sticks
JG

Pretzel Sticks

Notebook page 72
IB

Salzstangerl

3 gekochte Erdäpfel werden passiert mit so schwer Butter, Mehl und 1 Dotter vermischt und gesalzen, Stangerl geformt mit Ei bestriechen mit Salz und Kümmel bestreut.

Pretzel Sticks (Notebook page 72)

3 boiled potatoes are mashed and mixed with so heavy butter and flour and 1 yolk mixed and salted. Bake stick shapes brushed with egg, salted and sprinkled with caraway seeds.

Ingredients

- 3 potatoes (about 500g)
- 250g butter
- 500g flour (all purpose)
- 1 egg yolk
- 1 tsp salt
- Caraway seeds

Pretzel Sticks
JG

Instructions

1. Boil the potatoes until soft and when cold mash them with 1 egg yolk
2. Stir the softened butter until fluffy and add the flour, potatoes and salt
3. Mix well and knead thoroughly
4. Roll out the dough on a floured surface to about 0.5 " (1.2 cm) thickness
5. Create sticks or pretzels and lay on a parchment paper lined baking sheet
6. Brush with egg and sprinkle with salt and caraway seeds
7. Bake in 400°F (200°C) oven for 50 - 55 minutes

Crumbly Croissants

Notebook page 42
IB

Mürbe Kipferln
56dka Mehl wird mit 42dka Butter abgebröselt, dann mit 2 Eidotter, 2 Löffel sauren Rahm, 2 Löffel Wein und etwas salz zu einen etwas festeren Teig als zu einem Strudel geknetet und so wie ein butterteig behandelt. Nach zweimaligen Rasten ausgewalkt und mittelst eines heißen Messers in viereckige Stücke geschnitten, entweder mit Salse oder Nüsse gefüllt, in Form eines Kipfels zusammengerollt, oben mit ei bestrichen, und grob gehackte mandeln darauf gestreut und langsam gebacken, hernach mit Vanillezucker bestreut.

Crumbly Croissants (Notebook page 42)
560g flour is crumbled with 420g butter, then kneaded with 2 egg yolks, 2 spoons of sour cream, 2 spoons of wine and a little salt to make a dough that is a little firmer than a strudel dough and handled like a butter dough. After resting it twice, roll it out and cut it into square pieces with a hot knife, either fill it with marmalade or nuts, roll it up in the shape of a croissant, coat the top with an egg, and sprinkle coarsely chopped almonds on top and slowly bake it, then sprinkle it with vanilla sugar.

Ingredients

- 560g flour (all purpose)
- 420g butter (soft)
- 2 egg yolks
- 2 tbs sour cream
- 2 tbs white wine
- Salt
- Coarsely chopped almonds

Crumbly Croissant
JG

Instructions

1. Crumble the flour with the butter
2. Knead it with two egg yolks and 2 tbs of sour cream and 2 tbs wine until little firmer than a strudel dough and handle it like a butter dough
3. Let it rest two times, at least 20 minutes and knead the dough in between
4. Roll out the dough and cut into triangles. Add a spoonful of your choice of filling* and roll it up into a shape of croissant
5. Coat the top with an egg and sprinkle with coarsely chopped almonds
6. Bake in a preheated oven of 350°F (180°C) for about 25 minutes or until lightly brown

*Can be filled with walnuts, jam, poppy seeds or cheese, or without any filling

---

The **Crumbly Croissant** (*Mürben Kipfel*), is a crescent-shaped pastry, with generous amount of butter or lard and sometimes sugar and almonds.

According to tradition, the *kipfel* originated in 1683 to celebrate the Austrian victory over the Ottomans at the siege of Vienna. The story follows that a baker, up early to make bread, saved the city when he heard the Turks tunneling underneath the city and sounded an alarm. The *kipfel's* curved shape said to mimic the crescent moon of the Ottoman flag, to pay tribute to the resolute spirit of a city that resisted a powerful invading force.

Butter Scones

Notebook page 33
IB

Butter Pogatschen
28dka Butter, 2 drittel Liter Mehl mit dem Nudelwalken gut verarbeitet, 2 Eidotter etwas salz, ein großes Stück Schwein Schmalz, soviel Rahm, dass ein leichter teig daraus wird, gut ausarbeiten messerrückendick auswalken, zusammenlegen und dreimal rasten lassen. Es ist gut, wenn man dazwischen auch von einer Lemonie Saft gibt, dann walkt man den teig kleinfingerdick aus verziere mit dem Messer oben den Teig.

Butter Scones (Notebook page 33)
280gram butter, 2 thirds of a liter of flour processed well with the rolling pin, 2 egg yolks a little salt, a large piece of pork lard, enough cream to make a light dough. Work out well, roll out the thickness of the back of a knife, fold it up and let it rest three times. It's good if you add lemon juice in between, then roll the dough out as thick as your little finger and decorate the top with a knife.

Ingredients

- 2 egg yolks
- 150g butter (soft)
- 400g flour
- 1 tbs salt
- 50g lard
- 2-3 tbs sour cream (or as needed)
- Lemon juice
- Flour for dusting

Instructions

1. Combine the flour and the butter completely
2. Add egg yolks, lard and salt mix well
3. Add sour cream to make it a light dough and knead thoroughly
4. Roll out thinly, brush with lemon juice and fold it up. Let it rest for 30 minutes
5. Repeat 2 more times
6. Roll it out to a finger thick sheet and cut out scones with a round cookie cutter
7. Make a grid pattern, with a knife, on top of each and brush with an egg and sprinkle with salt
8. Bake in a preheated oven of 350°F (180°C) for 45 minutes

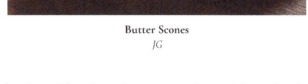

Butter Scones
JG

Pogache (scone) are round, salty pastries that are part of the typical cuisine of the Carpathian Basin (Pannonian Basin) – all of Hungary, but it also extends to Ukraine, Romania, Serbia, Croatia, Slovakia, Slovenia, and Austria. The name "Pannonian" comes from the province of the Roman Empire called Pannonia.

Butter Scones
JG

Butter scones (*pogácsa*) are a very common, popular savory pastry in Hungary, which, like the well-known lard scones, are only baked with lard instead of butter, and are offered in different variations in almost every bakery in Budapest in particular. These small bites are intended to be eaten either as finger food with wine or beer, but also as a small side dish with a soup or salad, or just because they taste so great as a snack in between.

("Ungarische Butterpogatschen". Mamas Rezepte. www.mamas-rezepte.de. 2022)

The name *pogache* is derived from the Latin word *foccantia* "baked dough".

10

Grandmother Ilona

ILONA BINETTER (ADLER)

1886 - 1976

Armin Adler and Family, 1903
JG

My grandmother was born as Ilka Adler on August 27, 1886, in Nagytapolcsány (Topoľčany), Slovakia, to parents Judith and Dr. Armin Adler. She had 6 siblings: One older sister, Elza, a younger brother Miksa, and 4 younger sisters Blanka, Hermina, Gizella and Paula. I think this was the order of birth of the children in her family.

Topoľčany was a typical smalltown in the Austro-Hungarian Empire, with quite a large Jewish population. At home they spoke both Hungarian and German, in the Austro-Bavarian dialect.

Her father, Armin, was a respected lawyer, member of the city's council, the regional legislature and member of the Board of Directors and attorney at the local Commercial and Credit Bank. He died on June 1, 1905, when my grandmother was 19, already married and expecting her first child.

Her mother, Judith, whom I am named after, was a widow for 24 years and died on July 4, 1929.

My grandmother married very young, on July 24, 1904. She married Fülöp Binetter, and they moved to his hometown of Nyitra, about 32 km from Topoľčany. My grandfather was an architect, and his family had a lumber wholesale business. .

Grandmother Ilona, 1904
JG

Their first child, Antal, my father, was born in 1905, just four days after the death of my great grandfather. They had two more sons Imre in 1907 and Gyula in 1909.

First born child, Antal, 1906
JG

Fülöp Binetter, 1904
JG

During WWI, my grandfather served in the Austro-Hungarian army somewhere in Albania. I have a collection of loving letters he wrote to his family and affectionate words to his wife. Those years must have been difficult for my grandmother, having to raise alone their teenage boys.

Nyitra, 1910
JG

With Mother and Husband,
Zilina, 1916
JG

After the end of the war and the dissolution of the Austro-Hungarian Empire their lives must have changed. Sometime, around 1917 the family moved to Budapest, after living a couple of years in Bratislava and Zilina.

Antal, Imre, Gyula, 1910
JG

The brothers, Bratislava 1920
JG

My father and his brothers were all grown up by the time they moved to Budapest. Between the two World Wars Budapest was a lively city and Jewish families were prosperous. My grandfather, Fülöp, established a company, *Herkules r.t., Joinery and Building Material Trading*, with his eldest son Antal (my father).

Their youngest son, Gyula, had a prominent position at an international trade company *Hoffer—Schrantz—Clayton—Shuttleworth Magyar Gépgyári Müvek Rt*, (Hungarian Machinery Works), until 1941.

Herkules r.t., 1928
JG

Binetter Gyula, Budapest 1940
JG

Opatia, 1928
JG

My grandparents had a relatively comfortable life, judging from photos taken at home and on vacations throughout Europe – holidays with friends in Opatia, Croatia, Nice and Monte Carlo in France, and ski in Italy.

Monte Carlo, Opera House, France
JG

With friends in Via Lattea, Claviere Italy, 1937
JG

Via Latea, Claviere, Italy, 1937
JG

It all ended with the anti-Jewish laws and measures, adopted by Hungary between 1938 and 1941, to exclude Jews from many professions, universities, and civil service. The laws reversed the equal citizenship status Jews had in Hungary since 1867.

Binetter Family, Budapest, 1927
JG

Nice, France
JG

Crystal Palace, Nice
JG

Life became very difficult with all the anti-Jewish laws issued by the Hungarian government after 1939. Two of the Binetter brothers were required for labour service in the infamous Labour Battalions. Until the German occupation of Budapest, in April 1942, life was relatively safe but then the deportations started.

Antal Binetter, my father, 1943
JG

The family went into hiding, some found refuge in a safe house outside the Jewish ghetto, having diplomatic protection by neutral politicians, and had Protective Passports on behalf of the Swedish Legation, issued by Raoul Wallenberg.

Swedish Legation Badge 1944
http://en.wikipedia.org/wiki/ User:Tamas_Szabo

Life during the rest of the war years was difficult but the family survived all the atrocities and the brutal battle over Budapest. Shortly after the end of the war my grandfather became sick with pneumonia. There was shortage of medications like penicillin to save him and he died in December 1945.

Binetter Fülöp

The news about the youngest brother, Gyula (Gyuszko), came later. He did not return from Russia, where he was deployed with the Jewish Labour Battalions, most likely, died in the harsh conditions of winter near Voronezh and the mistreatment of the German and Hungarian commanders or as a prisoner of war in Morshanks.

Grandfather's grave at the Rákoskeresztúri Cemetery
JG

Alone in Budapest my grandmother was also cut off from her siblings. Two of her sisters, Paula (Sòs) and Blanka (Tausz) and their families did not survive the Holocaust – they were murdered in one of the Nazi concentration camps. Her sister, Gisella and husband Siegfried (Kudelka) with their twin boys left Slovakia to Israel before the war. Miksa (Max) Adler immigrated to the US and Elza (Müller) was living in Zilina, Czech Republic. I could not find any information about her sister, Hermina (Biró).

By 1946, at the age of 57 my grandmother was a widow and soon had 2 grandchildren – my cousin Georges was born in Belgium, and I was born in Budapest. Grandmother was living in a Budapest suburb, sharing an apartment with Zimi (Zimmerman Laura). I never understood how Zimi was related to our family, but I used to see her when I was visiting my grandmother and liked her a lot. My visits with grandmother were joyful and I have happy memories from the short time I had her presence in my life.

With grandmother in Budapest Zoo, 1948, Zimi on the left and my mother on the right
JG

When I was 10 years old, right after the Hungarian Uprising of 1956, my parents and I fled from Hungary and with many other refugees ended up in Vienna on route to Israel and US. I never saw my grandmother again, but she kept in touch with me by letters and photos and on rare occasion over the phone.

Shortly after our departure from Budapest my grandmother applied for a visa to Belgium to join her son, Imre, and his family there. She lived in Belgium for the last 20 years of her life. I am not sure how her life was there, but I know that she was a realistic and practical person and managed to enjoy her new circumstances.

With Georges, Antwerp Belgium, 1959
JG

Just recently I learned more details about her life there while reading her letters to my father. She was a prolific letter writer and I learned about her extensive correspondence with her siblings, family and friends.

The letters stopped in the last two years of her life due to eyesight problems and just old age.

Grandmother with Imre, Antwerp 1965
JG

PASTRIES FROM THE PAST ~ 145

She died in Belgium in 1976. Among her possession was this recipe notebook.

Recipe Notebook
JG

ABOUT THE AUTHOR

Judith Gurfinkel is a Hungarian born enthusiastic baker who embarked on a project of reviving old Austro-Hungarian pastry recipes, triggered by a family inheritance. She launched *Pastries from the Past* as a book to bring new life into the hundred-year-old recipes. While writing the book she translated the German and Hungarian texts, converted them to current units of measures and ingredients, tried them out by baking and tasting and documenting step by step instructions and finally, by photographing the process and the results.

She lives in Vancouver, Canada and frequently prepares delicious cakes for her family and friends.

CPSIA information can be obtained
at www.ICGtesting.com
Printed in the USA
BVHW010320201222
654443BV00001B/1